I0418494

BEYOND BROKEN

JEFFREY GEURINK

Beyond Broken
by Jeffrey Geurink

Published by Rise Up Publishing

Paperback ISBN: 979-8-9909967-0-0
Copyright © 2025 by Jeffrey Geurink. All rights reserved.

Cover design by Jenneth Leed
Jennethleed.com

Publishing services by Ben Wolf, Inc.
www.benwolf.com/editing-services

Available in print and ebook format on amazon.com.

All rights reserved. Non-commercial interests may reproduce portions of this book without the express written permission of the author, provided the text does not exceed 500 words.

Commercial interests: No part of this publication may be reproduced in any form, stored in a retrieval system, or transmitted in any form by any means—electronic, photocopy, recording, or otherwise—without prior written permission of the author, except as provided by the United States of America copyright law.

All Scripture verses used within adhere to the guidelines of the respective rights holders for each version represented.

Printed in the United States of America.

Dedicated to Randall Geurink

1-20-2023. I lost my Superman… my hero … the most selfless man, with the most giving heart that would not hurt a soul. The hardest working man I have ever encountered on my time here on Earth. Shoes that I can only try to fill. Words cannot express the everlasting impact this man has left on me as well as everyone that had the chance to know him. May your legacy carry on through our family.

Addiction is very real and takes many from this life way too early. My father took me in his arms at the airport where I was boarding a flight to forever change my life…

His words to me in that moment: "You're more of a man than I will ever be… You reached out for help…"

You may have lost your fight, Pops, but I will carry on my message of recovery and hope to all those who are lost, broken and suffering. You won't get the chance to read this, but your passing was part of God's story through me. Rest easy, Pops, and until we meet again…

"FLY HIGH WITH THE EAGLES"

CONTENTS

MY STEP 1

POWERLESS OVER ALCOHOL

On September 17th, 2020, an older gentleman at the 11am meeting at Adventure Church stated, "As alcoholics, when we aren't drinking, we are wishing we were drunk, and once we are drunk, we are praying we were sober."

This hit home hard with me, especially in the later part of my illness. I couldn't wait to get that first drink sliding down my throat, and the poison connecting all the dots in my hurting mind, body, and soul.

It was as if my truck was on autopilot to one of three gas stations. Of course, I wouldn't always hit the same one. I wouldn't want them thinking I had a "drinking problem." Even if I drank so much and blacked-out, not knowing what I had done the night before, that somehow against my will was another purchase and feeling of remorse.

I didn't really want to drink, but it controlled me, my emotions, and my physical and emotional pains. I was in a vicious cycle that was killing me. I was angry at the world, angry at God, and I was ready to give away what little I had and give up on everything in this life that I had created in self-will.

My life had compiled many problems that I couldn't solve through my own will. I was powerless to alcohol, and it dictated every move I made. Hell, most of the times, getting alcohol and consuming it was the only action I would pull off for days.

At the end of every drunken binge, I would hit my knees and pray for God's strength to make me a better man, father, son, and everything I could be. My life had evolved into anxiously awaiting my next binge, not just having a couple drinks to de-stress for the day. It was typically all-day s*** shows, for the most part. I would start at 8AM, be drunk by 1PM, sleep till 7PM, and be drinking again by 8PM until my mind shut down or my body gave up. It got to where my body couldn't function without alcohol.

Most times I wouldn't eat, and if I tried to eat first thing, I would vomit. Hell, most of the times I would throw up on my first drink. Hunched over the sink, body rejecting the poison, but convincing myself it was nerves, and two beers later I was sitting in my sweet spot. If it wasn't for the stimulus check I would have drunk myself out of home, work, and life. It supported my raging addiction.

I was only so lucky that, in complete desperation, and reaching out to my ex-wife, I took a leap of faith and hopped a plane to California. I self-admitted into a rehabilitation center. I was leaving everything behind me to focus on fixing me. Turning the keys to my life over to God, and some group of workers to straighten out my life. I wanted to find purpose and step away from the drink. I wanted to regain control of myself and my life.

As I look back, I could never just have a few drinks and stop. If I bought 6, I drank 6. If I bought 12, I drank 12. If I bought 30 for the weekend, I wouldn't stop until I shutdown mentally or physically. Normally to wake up to four beers left in the 30-beer box, with the first thought of the day being my planning to get enough to make it through another day.

Sometimes I, "tricked myself," into acting like I could drink responsibly by just having a few beers and heading home. Yet that craving was there, and the next stop was a gas station to buy way more than I needed to have. "One more," as a "night cap." To find myself reaching for the last beer in the box as I staggered though the house drinking every last drop before passing out.

While married and staying super active the problem was there, but not as unmanageable, and my ex-wife kept me overly busy. Once divorce hit and I was left to my own devices.... It was game over! I didn't want to feel, and my best friend, Alcohol, was there to save the day.

What once drowned away the work week or that gal who cheated me or did me wrong, became something far more severe. It wasn't fun and rebellious anymore... it was physically drowning me. Suffocating my life... Without it, I couldn't breathe. All at the same time, it was slowly killing me day by day, drink by drink.

What was once fun-filled nights had turned into OWIs, drinking other people's stashes, and waking up to be drug through a home by cops, not knowing where I was at. I had broken relationships with friends and family, and burning these bridges left me completely isolated. I had maxed out credit cards and I hated my job that I was in terrible standing with.

I was falling over in drunken stupors. One time giving myself a black eye, and one time smacking the back of my head falling out of the shower. I would then lie my way through it. I was not showering or eating for 3-5 days and putting back on work clothes to go buy more alcohol... Had to make myself look productive. To the last night, cashing 18 beers, getting in my truck, and praying to God to let me get to the gas station one last time... If that isn't powerless and unmanageable to alcohol... then I don't know what it is!

MY STEP 2

RESTORE ME TO SANITY

For this accumulation of uncontrollable self-will... I surrender!!! I give up!!! I give in!!! My will alone cannot and will not lead to a meaningful life of purpose. I give the keys to my life over to the God of my understanding. I will serve you and walk in your will. Seeking to fulfill spiritual progress over spiritual perfection.

Although I am a man of many great and grand ideas, for some reason alcohol had to show its face. Once shown, it was completely my way, and this is how it's going to be, and this is how it works. Just so happens my ideas never came to fruition, and it was few and far between, if one came to any good.

When alcohol took total control over me it was complete insanity. It thought for me. If it was for me to regain sanity, it wasn't going to be on my terms. An outside power had to present itself to me. For left to my own devices, it was alcohol that was the answer to all my problems. I knew they weren't being fixed, but I was hooked to the numbing feeling. I didn't want to feel or deal with the world I had created that I was so angry with.

Many nights in a drunken haze, I would let hot water cascade down my body as I fell to my knees... "Dear Lord, give me the strength to be a better man… Dear Lord, let me stop the drinking that is killing me…"

And on July 8th, 2020, I boarded a plane and was off to sober up. Handing the keys to my life to complete strangers on a leap of faith. Leaving my kids and family behind on a mission to redeem my life.

MY STEP 3

TURNING MY WILL OVER

It was in taking this leap of faith, that I was surrendering my will. A scary and humbling day. As I hugged my children, parents, sister, and ex-wife goodbye… with a mustard seed of faith, I was turning over my life to God's will. I hugged my son and said, "Don't worry, Bud. I will be good."

Then I thought to myself, "You know what, Son?" and said, "I will come back better… not just good!"

I left with the mind set of **NO TURNING BACK!** I no longer wanted the life I was living. I had reached that "**Gift Of Desperation,**" that you hear spoken of in the rooms of AA. My will just straight up sucks, or should I say the lack of will.

I had all the brains and natural talent in the world. I trained myself to adapt to any situation thrown at me. Yet left to my own devices, I would drink it all away to a 12 ounce can that I bought… yet it owned me. I was more than ready and needed a new design for living before my life was gone.

Although many years before that I had accepted Christ as my savior, I had never got to know him. In the free will that God gives us, I not only took off in it and all the blessings I received but gave no thanks and brought myself to some of the darkest places I had ever been in my life, and in this, I was humbled.

PROLOGUE

S taring off over the immaculate L.A. skyline... F***ing Hollywood! Mountains surrounded me as I mingled in awe with fellow group members. Absolutely stunning! Where dreams were made, but I came to find out, where even more were crushed. Million-dollar homes with private pools. It was what one would see in the movies, and I was standing smack dab in the middle of it.

Never thought that my poor decisions would have me living my own Hollywood movie scene... But here I was! Hollywood sign to my right with the Griffith Observatory on my left. In the far distance, you could see the massive, new L.A. Rams stadium. The air was crisp, and the sun was bright. It was like a desert-mountain oasis. The tech informed me I was lucky for COVID timing. Otherwise, we'd be sucking pollution haze down our windpipes.

To think, just ten short days ago I was lying down in panic mode. My anxiety was on full blast, coming off a late-night bender. 26-beer cans scattered across my living room floor... what normally would sedate a person only had me wanting more... and more. I just couldn't drink enough to kill my anxieties.

So low in life, and in an act of desperation, I reached out to my ex-wife... My EX-WIFE! The one I put huge blame on for destroying me. I was killing myself... The next thing you know, I was on a conference call. Thoughts running crazy in my head as I was ready to lose or risk it all.

Luckily with my ex-wife's stern push to regain control and use my resources available through the job (I hated) to get help, I self-admitted into rehab. I booked a flight to California that would forever change my life. Tired, scared, frustrated, depressed, and filled with anxiety. I had lost control and was taking a leap of faith. I was **<u>BEYOND BROKEN.</u>** There was **<u>NO TURNING BACK</u>**

PART I
NO TURNING BACK:
MY RECOVERY JOURNEY

THE CALIFORNIA CHRONICLES

Nervous and scared... I was filled with anxiety coming off a heavy night of binge drinking. I woke early with all sorts of energy and thoughts running through my head. I started texting my ex-wife, (out of all people), at six-something in the morning. My thoughts were racing and scattered, trying to decide what to do.

Do I quit my job??? I hated it, anyway. Cash-out my 401k and start new??? Or do I go back to work and probably get fired, anyway? My mind wasn't slowing down. As much as I didn't give two f**ks about anything, I still cared, deep down. My ex-wife managed to pull off a conference call that would soon bring into realization... Do it, Jeff! Jump! Take that leap of faith.

In sorting things out, I didn't realize just how fast things were happening. Stay working, but go on short-term disability, use insurance to get good help, and then decide my next move was what the admissions, my ex-wife, and I came to agree on.

"So, you want to fly out tomorrow?" came from the admissions person.

"Ughhh? No... How about Friday, instead?"

"Well, how about Wednesday?"

My ex-wife chimed in on the three-way call, "Jeff, do you want this?"

"Yeah, I want this!" I proclaimed.

She replied, "Then fly out Wednesday. Don't worry about stuff. We will make sure you're covered."

I agreed to Wednesday... So, I guess I was making the jump... taking the leap of faith... IN TWO DAYS!!!!! AHHHHH!!! Holy hell scramble, but hey... why not procrastinate? I figured to take the rest of the day to get drunk one last time and let go of that way of life. So that's exactly what I did for the day. It was a sense of relief, for damn sure.

After an 18 pack of Busch Lattes, I got to letting my alcoholic mind wander. Was that enough beers or should I grab another sixer of tall boys? My mind battling itself, as usual.

"Ahhhhh, you're good, Jeff…"

"Nah, go grab the sixer…"

"But what if I get pulled over???"

"Ahhhhh, God knows I'm getting sober. Just go for it!"

So, I hopped in the truck, fresh off slamming 18 beers, thinking that 6 more tall boys were exactly what I needed. Before leaving my parking space, I looked up and prayed to God to let the cops be elsewhere. Somehow, I pulled it off. Maybe a little bit of grace.

After an eventful day of slamming beers and playing Xbox, I got a text from Jay O. from Admissions as I started into my sixer of tall boys. We started conversing about kids, life, and gaming. He, too, was a recovered addict and a new dad.

It was a good feeling knowing in taking this leap that I just met a cool guy. As I'm chugging down my beers from the sixer, Jay let me know that not many people get accepted to Rise Up Recovery, and that someone must be watching over me. This was a great feeling, knowing I was going to be in good hands.

With a few beers left from my sixer, I hopped on Xbox Live one last time. I knew Big Mike would be on. As I finished my 26th beer for the day, I decided I had enough and signed-off. I took myself to my couch and drifted off to sleep. I was not so nerve-filled, knowing I made the right decision.

7 – 7 – 20: (Tuesday): *The Scramble:*

I t wouldn't be a normal day without waking up to a phone call with a pounding headache. It was my daughter.

"Hey, Dad! When ya picking us up?"

"Ahhhhh… Was just getting ready to head that way."

"Okay! See ya soon!"

So now pull yourself together, dumb s**t. You told your kids 9AM, and it's 9:30 and you're still laying on the couch drunk from last night's binge. I hopped up and decided to shower quickly so I didn't reek of booze. So 10:30AM rolls around and I'm just leaving the apartment.

As usual, I take the back long way because my head is all disoriented and vision is fuzzy. All this time thinking to myself, one more good reason to make the jump. Hell, lying to my kids about pick-up times because I can't pick up my own worthless self, and then trying to navigate with a cloudy mind.

I finally made it to the kids' mom's house around 11AM, and to my luck, I was met by the kids' mother.

"How ya feeling?"

"F**king scared… I don't know."

"It will be good for you."

"Yes, I know. Here's where I will be at. (I show her pics of Rise Up.)

"Well, heck! Can I come, too?"

My daughter got to the vehicle and small chat continued.

"Where is the boy?"

"I don't know. I Facetimed him."

Another five minutes went by and out staggers the boy.

"You just wake up? I told you to go to bed early."

"Yeah… I went to bed at 5AM."

"Nice…"

Not that I can say much, being two hours late and a terrible role model as of the moment. As we went to leave, Tara mentioned that all the guys she had kids with ended up in rehab or messed up. She confided in herself that she wasn't the problem. She always was a self-centered bi… and makes one wonder why she isn't getting any help, but… Off we go!

I had the son drive (probably safer, anyway.) We stopped at Wal-Mart to grab some last-minute essentials off my pack list. Like masks, because Lord knows I will need those for no reason. I went in the store alone because the kids wanted to stay in the truck.

Hung-over like no other, I bobbed and weaved through the store. I tried gathering my thoughts to remember what I needed, but I was still too drunk to clear my mind. I felt like death and wanted to just fall over. Somehow, I pulled it off and we were homebound.

As usual, the son snuck off to his room and the daughter plopped down on the couch and started binging Netflix. I tried to pull myself together and refocus. Time to get busy, Jeff! You leave tomorrow! I went into Rambo mode. I did dishes, swept the floors, cleaned the bathroom, put clothes away, disinfected everything, and tried to have everything in place for my return home. My sister told me she was going to clean it when I left, but I had to stay busy and distracted.

Once that was all done, now it was the dreadful work call. I had reached out to my business rep, and he advised me to just be honest, but to not go into detail. I sent an email to HR and a text to the HR manager, and I also called the call-in line. HR then called me back in a conference call. Nervous, I briefly stated I would be on a leave of absence due to personal…

"Madison! Turn that damn phone down! This is important!" (She gave me a terrified look.)

…Due to personal reasons. For the first time, I felt at ease speaking with HR, and they were actually quite helpful. They informed me what to do and gave me peace of mind that my job was secure.

Knowing I had told myself I wouldn't get hammered before

my flight on Wednesday, it was still early and all of my ducks, for the most part, were in a row.

"Hey, Maddy, I said I wouldn't be getting hammered, but I got that "one last hoorah" feeling."

"Wouldn't blame ya, Dad."

So as usual, I let the alcohol make my decisions for me. I hopped in the truck and headed on my normal run to the gas station. I grabbed two bags of sunflower seeds, a 2 liter of Mt. Dew, and a 12 pack of Busch Lattes. You know, a good buzz, but not s**t-hammered, and get to bed early. Even though I knew parents were coming up for Mexican food and margaritas.

I didn't last two minutes through the door and.... Buschhhhhhhh!!!

The boy had fallen asleep, and the daughter was in her Zen space. I stood in the kitchen pacing, and time to time mumbling to myself. Cracking beer after beer, I looked at the time. Nine beers in and there was a knock at the door. It was my mom and dad.

To my last three beers... I handed one to my mom and one to my dad. We shared a "Cheers!" and made small talk. My mother went in to talk to my son, and he was in a mood. "Oh, woe is me!" because I had called him an idiot for doing 135mph in a car with his friends, in which the car had expired tags, and he had no license. His newfound freedom of life... He is a man! He makes his own rules, regardless of established laws.

It took Grandma sweet-talking him, but he finally decided to go along and eat. We piled in the car and took off for Eldridge. It wasn't long before we were seated at a table.

"What to drink, sir?"

"Lime margarita, blended and jumbo!"

As we finished up our meals, guess who needed another jumbo margarita. Dad ended up helping me drink it, but it was all good because I was feeling pretty good.

When we got back home, we parted ways, and my parents said they would see me tomorrow. Since the boy was in a better mood, and I was, too, I re-approached him about the car. I told him I'm leaving him so I could get better and that I didn't want to worry about getting a call that my son had been in a fatal car accident.

I asked him if what he did was a good idea. He agreed his actions weren't smart. I said, "You're not an idiot, but your actions were completely reckless, and I got to be Dad sometimes and not always a friend." I brought him in for a hug, and we traded "I love you's."

He then took off for his room with his sunflower seeds. After about six waters, a CBD gummy, and an eventful day texting family and friends about my decision, I decided to call it a night. I laid down my head, knowing I needed to be ready for the flight that would change my life.

7 – 8 – 20: (Wednesday): *Now Boarding*:

Anxiety must have gotten the best of me because I woke up a wrecking ball of nerves and no hangover. First thought that came to my mind was to take a hot shower to wake up and calm the nerves. I turned the water as hot as it would go. Due to apartment living, it was barely hot enough to fog up the mirror above the sink, but I had every intention of running it ice cold.

About 15 minutes into the shower, a weird feeling hit me, and I gagged. For the next three minutes, I aggressively dry heaved. I finally pulled my s**t together and decided I had had enough shower, and it was time to get out. I guess nerves got the best of me this fine morning at 8:15AM, and I still had a full day of anxiety to deal with.

Of course, both my kids stayed up late, which they normally do. But then again, knowing I was leaving, I'm sure they had a lot on their minds, too. I resorted to drill sergeant mode, and it was "Let's get moving, people." They weren't really having it, but my ex-wife was to pick us up at 8:45AM. They eventually got moving and she pulled up right on time.

Of course, Curtis, my 15-year-old, was dragging ass like crazy, but I finally got him out the door. As I slowly turned the deadbolt on the apartment door, I told myself, "**NO TURNING BACK!**" I loaded my belongings into the trunk of my ex-wife Amanda's car, and we piled in. We hit Casey's for a quick breakfast, and we were Cedar Rapids bound.

I remembered to save one anxiety medication, to try to keep my composure until I got to California. I had 30 pills from when I divorced two years ago, and in the last couple weeks went through all the pills but that one. I popped it at 10AM, knowing my nerves would be going haywire. I still was sitting on a buttload of CBD gummies, but I wanted to save those.

We pulled into an empty airport, other than a few stragglers here and there. After checking in my bags, I went back to talk with my kiddos. Next thing, I felt my nipples being twisted off my chest. As I turned around, there stood my sister and parents to greet me with hugs. It was a warming feeling that was definitely needed. Small talk burned time, and I almost forgot to call Admissions, but I remembered, and they said to call when I landed in Dallas, Texas.

The gang moved their way to the security check, and it got "REAL EMOTIONAL, REAL FAST." Tight hugs and kisses and tears filled everyone's eyes. I tried to stay strong but the whole leap of faith set in the vulnerability. Superman met his kryptonite. I squeezed everyone tight, but I will never forget what my father said to me. He told me that he was proud of me, and that I was much more a man than he was because I reached out for help, and he never did.

I gave my son and daughter one last hug as I bid farewell. I turned and headed for Security. The first look back, they all stood watching with eyes full of tears. The second time I looked back after entering Security, they were gone.

This was it, **<u>NO TURNING BACK!</u>** I can do this and I'm not alone. Now airplanes and I don't get along, but I knew I couldn't drink. (Which, typically, I was three rum and Cokes in before boarding.) Must have been the anxiety meds because I was feeling pretty good and accomplished with myself.

They called out boarding and I was group 8. It went fast, beings it was a small plane with 1/3 occupancy, due to this COVID agenda. Fortunately, I got to sit by a window, which is a must for me when flying. So many feelings and emotions were zinging through my brain waves. As the plane left the runway, all I could do was watch myself drift into the unknown. Not to mention, this was my first-time flying solo and sober.

The flight went smooth, but it was very quiet and sort of gloomy. People's faces covered in masks, due to some political agenda scare tactic. Being another election year, what else could possibly go wrong in 2020? People's tensions were already high, and being empathic, I just tried to pray and stay calm. As we descended from the air, I looked out at the massive city of Dallas, Texas.

I remembered loving the Dallas airport, but the last time I was here, I was hammered. I was with my sister on a one-way plane ticket to Las Vegas. We about missed our hub flight because we plopped down at a bar and got to having quite the good time. Just so happens this time I was alone, a nervous wreck, and sober!

I got off the plane to an ear-piercing siren and blue lights flashing all over. The people in the airport all looked disturbed and confused. I guess it was just an open-door alarm that was activated, but it was soon silenced… Phew!!!

So, I was originally supposed to have an hour layover when I got to Dallas. I took a quick piss and thought about grabbing lunch. I took a quick look at my boarding passes… boarding at 2:25PM. I checked my cell phone. Oh, s**t! It was already 2:00PM and I didn't know how to read my boarding pass.

I frantically looked around. I ended up spotting a concierge. The kind man pointed me to an Amtrak deal and told me to get off at C1. So, I did just that and ran into two employees when I got off. Just my luck, they could barely speak English and told me to ask a pilot. Just so happens one was walking by in quite a hurry, but politely he slowed down to help point me in the right direction.

I was at C12 and had to be at C2, which wasn't too far. Just the fact I was five minutes from boarding time, and I was hungry. So, in barely making it in time, I come to find out they delayed boarding by twenty minutes for maintenance work. I hit the nearest snack hub and grabbed peanut M&M's and some original Gardetto's. Not really what I was hungry for, but it added to the two granola bars I had eaten earlier.

I called the admission people again and they just told me to let them know when I boarded. Well, about ten mini-delays later and stealing parts off another plane, they finally let us board. I called Admissions again and they said to call again when I landed in Los Angeles, California.

This flight was a bit different. It was a jumbo jet packed elbow-to-elbow with people. Somehow, I got lucky and landed a window seat again. I thought it to be a one-hour flight, but we lost two hours in time zone change. The flight ended up being a two-hour-and-forty-minutes. Before take-off, I popped a good dose of CBD gummies, just to keep the nerves in check. You got this, Jeff, **NO TURNING BACK!**

While on the flight, the older lady next to me was kind enough to carry on a conversation. It made the last hour of the flight fly by. We talked about where we were from and where we were headed. She and her husband were off to see their son for his birthday. I fibbed a little and said I was on a personal retreat to a luxury resort. Next thing you know, we were descending.

Once we got off the plane, I was straight to the bathroom. I once again reached out to Admissions. Within minutes, I got a text from a guy named Edward, informing me he was waiting in Baggage Claim. Now where the heck is Baggage Claim? I went down a long, isolated hallway and reached a door that stated, "No Re-Entry." I guess this was it… **NO TURNING BACK!**

Looking around, confused, a tattoo-covered gent raised his hand and asked, "You Jeff?"

"Yes, sir!" I replied.

His name was Edward. We made a little small talk and headed to the parking garage. He informed me it was about a 45-minute drive to the recovery home. We approached a big, dirty, white 12 passenger van. If I wasn't getting hauled off to be murdered, I guess the van would suffice, and off we went through the streets of Los Angeles, California.

I was 110% chill, thanks to CBD, and was just soaking up the scenery. I made it to L.A., and I was sober. Not one drink all day. As the drive got closer to our destination, I asked Edward where the ocean was at. He gave me a puzzled look and answered not too close to us.

We then pulled up to a place that wasn't what I saw in the pictures. Ummmm?!?!? Where am I??? I had been texting the ex-wife saying I was good. Last text I got off was, "I'm not where I'm supposed to be!" before they yanked my phone. I was suddenly not so at ease and the dishonesty of being scammed set in.

A little bit (A LOT) confused, I decided to roll with the punches. The staff seemed pretty cool. They were a group of younger guys that had been through the program. I found out Edward had only been working with the company for a few weeks. I had to fill out a bunch of forms and answer a bunch of random questions. It wasn't seeming to be too legit, but until I figured out what was going on, it would have to do. It seemed as if I was at a safe haven with a nursing staff.

I was then asked to do a breathalyzer and piss test. They also made me change my clothes. I asked Edward if he wanted me to drop-trou, but he seemed cool with me staying in my drawers. They then took me to Nursing for a rapid COVID test, or maybe that was before... All I remember is I passed whatever rapid test they gave me.

I was then put in some small, stank room with some dude who was passed out. Oyyyy... "What in the f**k?" ran through my head. I was exhausted from a long day and the one dude ordered me a New York Steamer from Firehouse Subs. The nurse had given me two melatonin, and I was not sure what it would do to me. I guess they are to help with falling to sleep, and Lord knows I could use some good Z's.

As I laid there, completely uncomfortable, roomed up with someone I didn't know, coming down off whatever their crutch was, tears started to fill my eyes. So, Jeff... This is where your addiction has led you. Every feeling of failure and remorse ran through my brain as I struggled to hold onto the fact I was going to get better. On top of it, I was in some dog s**t bed in a hot room. This wasn't where I was supposed to be. God, why me???

Side note: my vitals were, like, 122/79, and all the people I encountered that were being treated all greeted me. So, everything seemed to be chill so far. I guess that was the vibe people got from me, too. I guess most problem drinkers came in wasted and belligerent. I tend to be a chill, fun-loving and caring guy, so that was a plus. Well, typically, but lately I had been full of fear and hate.

7 – 9 – 20: (Thursday): *Settling In:*

I tossed and turned in the piece-of-s**t bed with the crappy pillow most of the night. This definitely wasn't the five-star place from the pictures I saw online. I saw daylight poking through, so I decided to get up and moving for the day. Dude in the other bed was still zonked out. I'm not sure what he was on, or in for, but they had definitely gotten him sedated.

I gathered my stuff and made my way outside. I was met by the night shift crew and no one else moving. "BRRRR!!!" Was it ever chilly outside. So glad I thought California would be hot in July, and I chose to not pack any warm clothes. I guess I was still on Iowa time. It was 5AM, but to me it seemed like 7AM.

I went to the kitchen for a bite to eat. I grabbed a yogurt, banana, and a granola bar. I washed breakfast down with some orange juice, and then made my way back outside. I looked to the right and saw an older lad sitting under a cabana. I proceeded over to strike up a conversation.

His name was Todd. He was mid-50's and in for alcohol. I came to find out it was his third time at the facility. Guess he was like the father figure of rehab. He told me my roommate's name was John, and he was a cool guy. I guess that gave me a sense of ease.

Todd was from Michigan, and I also met Melvin. He, too, was from Michigan. A late-40's black man with a powerful voice. Being from the Midwest, I guess we wake up earlier. What was go time for us was sleep time for the snowflakes. It wasn't bad, though, because it was quiet and peaceful.

The next people I recall coming out for coffee and cigarettes were Angie and Charley. Angie, too, was in for alcohol. I came to find out she had fallen downstairs and had brain surgery, and then she went on a bender. She was a fun-loving gal, the mom of the house (AKA: Mama Bear), and then there was Charley... crazy and older grandma of the house. She was 90 pounds soaking wet,

COPD, smoked like a chimney, and had a raspy voice and huge smile. Charley was also in for alcohol.

Most of the early morning was a meet-and-greet. Others had groups and other stuff. I tried figuring out why I was in East Hollywood instead of Rise Up, but I was more or less brushed off and told it was being investigated. I was "sober," and "safe," but still uneasy about the whole housing situation.

Lunch came around and I was introduced to JoJo. Damn, could this guy throw down in the kitchen. He was a self-taught master chef and seemed to be a pretty chill guy. First meal was pork skewers and some squash that was seasoned perfectly. Safe to say I wouldn't go hungry, and more than grateful for this dude in the kitchen. I also ate kale salad and couscous. Food was fire!

I don't remember supper this day, beings I started writing these journals on 7-11-20. So, if you can bear with me until I get up to date. Overall, I was settling in and I'm a hard one to shake or break so I stayed pretty easy-going. All I know is **NO TURNING BACK.** If I start something, I need to finish it and do it to the best of my ability.

Well, shoot, now recalling the day, I do remember what JoJo whipped up for supper. I actually remember a lot more than I thought. Supper was a team building life skill day with JoJo. We prepped a killer meal. Belinda and I cut veggies and fruit, and I made a homemade whipped cream. Angie made some awesome chocolate chip cookies, Tom prepped shrimp, and one guy chopped fruit for the next day.

Once everything was all prepared, we moved to the "girls' house" because they had a bigger table with a dining room. Shrimp Alfredo, grilled asparagus, grilled peaches with fresh whipped cream, and a salad. How could I even forget a meal like that? It was good food with new acquaintances.

With full bellies, we all huddled around a small gas fireplace-thing and wound down for the night. As for my health, I was doing pretty well. I had no shakes or many withdrawal symptoms. Headaches and anxiety were my only real issues. I stayed on top of my blood pressure and tried not to worry too much. Just relax, have faith, and trust the process.

I never did get my telephone call. Just promises for another day. Well, wait, I did call Amanda, scratch that, it was Friday. No, it was today I got my one safe call during blackout period. I let Amanda know I was safe, but I wasn't where I was told I was going. I told her to let everyone know I was doing well.

Anyways, Nursing had my back, and Cheryl... I forgot about that group. She was our head therapist and, damn, was she beautiful. I actually spoke up in groups, too. The group was about forgiveness. Not that I'm one to have scattered thoughts (Ha, Ha, Ha), but in being sober I realized the thoughts came back to me. So, I guess I'll wrap things up on that note.

Forgiveness is something I've struggled with in the past. I say it, but I don't believe it, and it ends up haunting me. I guess not all the time, but in certain situations, I have let it keep me from moving forward. In this, I hope to let what is be and change what I have the power to. To let go of things I can't change and forgive not only others, but myself as well. That in cleaning my side of the street, I can move forward in the future, being a better me.

A nother normal start to the morning. I woke up early again and hit the guys' house for breakfast. This morning it was a yogurt, banana, and a bowl of Trix. I washed down breakfast with orange juice and grabbed an ice water. I decided to start drawing and got a doodle pad to do my drawings for the day. It keeps my mind busy and shifts my focus.

I'm never real sure what I am going to draw, either. I look at it as documenting my journey of sobriety and giving people an insight of my complex brain. To no surprise, the morning gang pulled together. We had Todd, Melvin, Angie, and then out stumbles Charley. The alcoholic morning squad was all there. Other than Melvin; I think he was in for crack. The heavy drug users seemed to like their sleep. That or it was the sedation meds, but I'm no doctor.

My drawing of the day was a down arrow above the word "FEAR" in fire, with fire under it. I had a notion to draw around words that described my feelings. Words that related to my journey. The first drawing I did was the word "faith" in a cross. Well, it was actually the entry into the girls' house, but that page ripped out. My daughter's name, "Madison," was the next drawing.

Once the spooks woke up, we all got our meds before first Group. My meds so far have been Vitamin B1, B6, B12, and CBD gummies. I did take a few ibuprofens as well, but for the most part, staying away from pills. I didn't come to get hooked on some other s**t. I guess I did get some melatonin the first night, but definitely not the same meds that most of the people were on. It's odd I can only get my "meds" at 8AM or after. I didn't realize there was a specific time to take vitamins, but I guess it is what it is. **NO TURNING BACK!**

The first group of the day was with Becca. She is quiet, shy, and innocent. She seems a bit scared, being new, but I hope the best for her. People raced to the snack box for fruit snacks and chips before plopping down on the couches. Which I came to realize that groups were hard for addicts to sit still in. All these fidgety and restless lost souls digging thru chip bags, and constantly getting up and moving around.

One thing I learned in life is to listen to understand, not to reply. So, in groups, I try to hear out the speaker, plus take in full what others say. A lot of the addicts are lost in their own minds, and they are thinking about everything but what's being talked about in groups. It's their sobriety journey, so it is what they make of it.

The group topic today was, "GRATITUDE." After a short reading, there were six questions asked to us all. I will now share the questions and my responses to them. Not that I understood fully what I was writing, but at the time how I perceived the questions and my quick response during the group session.

Q1) When I felt scared or hurt, how did my parents address my emotions?

A1) My dad would say it didn't hurt me a bit. My mom was more attentive. She was like the therapist and the nurse. A sense of Nature-vs-Nurture.

Q2) When something "BIG" happened in my house, was there communication?

A2) From what I remember, my parents sheltered us from what was going on. They kept us safe, and they stayed together and worked things out.

Q3) What messages did I get around who I was or who I was supposed be?

A3) I was raised to work hard and be a good person. Also, to take personal responsibility for my actions. My parents were more practical, so they didn't really emphasize pursuing passion.

Q4) What activities or actions did I take part in to receive love or approval?

A4) Sports, working at age 12, buying my own stuff. I made gifts, which ties into the 5 love languages. You tend to give love how you want to receive it.

Q5) Were there secret things we didn't speak about or things we hid from the public?

A5) All the illegal shenanigans we pulled, shooting the neighbor's dog with BB guns. Our feelings on life and how we perceived it. As for parents, it was pretty open book.

Q6) Did I feel free to be myself or did I fear the reactions of my family?

A6) Mom tried laying down the law, but Dad raised us to be independent, hard-working kids that knew right from wrong, and to accept consequences for poor decisions. Dad would never let us fall completely, though. I was the outlandish, outspoken middle child. For the most part I stayed to myself, but Dad would do what he could to help us pursue things in life.

The meeting ended before I was able to share, but it was all good. I remember the therapist Stefany spoke, but I don't recall much. I do remember JoJo bringing in bacon cheeseburgers and sweet potato fries for lunch... DAMN! This boy is going to get fat up in this joint!

I found out through conversation with JoJo that he didn't go to culinary school. He was taught under a master chef. His teacher told him that he didn't need to go to school. I completely agree.

He was a hard-working man, with passion for food, and knowledge of the kitchen. I'm trying to make mental notes on his twists on recipes. I think he must have heard me Thursday when I said I was from Iowa and loved bacon and steak. Kudos, my man! Keep bringing the fire dishes.

Now onto "The Boss." I finally got to talk to Stefany. Won't lie, but first impression was a Cali-snowflake-liberal-snob, which, so far, my judgment isn't too far off. In expressing my concerns, all it came down to her was, "Why does it matter?" Here ya go, Stefany… It matters to me! Case closed! It was my sobriety, and I was lied to about where I was going.

We got someone from Rise Up on the phone, and he said I was fully funded to go to Rise Up. Hmmmm??? Interesting… We then called Amanda (The Boss.) Amanda expressed her concerns, and we shared text and emails with Stefany. It was like I was unfolding some weird insurance rehab scam.

Amanda was at her daughter's basketball game but said she would be on it ASAP. I totally believed it, too. Amanda was a case manager, and a damn good one. Not the person you want investigating your company. The conversation ended flustered, and we separated ways. Now these assholes were dealing with "The Boss!"

Before the next group session, I went to Nursing. I could feel the anxiety setting in. They gave me some 50mg green-and-white pill. I can't remember what it was called. When I got to Group, I leaned forward in my chair. I put my hands together, I took a deep breath, and I gave it to God. **NO TURNING BACK!**

After praying, I came to senses with my surroundings. An older black man named Darrell sat laid-back in a chair. A powerful speaker with a fun-loving, but straightforward approach. He turned his talk to Robby. Robby was a repeat rehabber, in on heroin. At 25 years old, he had already been to rehab over 20 times. Hepatitis and God only knows what other diseases. Kid knew his drugs, for damn sure, and could have been a pharmacist.

Darrell went in on him, and I got to feeling bad for the kid. All strung out on meds, coming down off the hard s**t, and he was hugging a pillow, crying. Darrell ended up asking if he was being too hard. You could tell he struck a nerve with the kid that made him think on life. We then watched a YouTube stream about a guy, 15 years sober, that started a company that was the fastest to become a Fortune 500 company.

It was a TED Talk that related being a business owner to being an addict. It made a lot of sense, and showed that our pasts don't define our futures, but our struggles are necessary to understand, appreciate, and have gratitude and humility for our successes.

When Group Chat got to me after the video ended, I knew it would be hard for me. Already a ball of emotions, I choked out the word "authenticity." I stated even Superman falls and that I found my kryptonite. Hugging my kids goodbye, I had to show vulnerab… Vulnerability! I choked up but finally got the word out.

Darrell then stated, "See, this is real. Good share, my man! Good share! You choked up just trying to get it out. Good stuff!"

Group ended and all I remember next was the smell of grilled chicken. JoJo had done it again. It was suppertime. Caribbean jerk chicken legs with black beans and rice. Man can season some food. Damn, were those some good chicken legs.

Before I forget, Happy Birthday, brother! Hope you had a good one! We then fizzled out with our bellies all stuffed. We lit a fire and made small chat under the cabana. That was, until the spooks came alive. Cheyenne, a meth and alcohol addict with no teeth, and the new pink-haired chick, Kristin, went berserker mode. This Kristin chick is something else. Young and very disrespectful, acting like the world owes her something. Claiming to be a lesbian, but she slept with men for drug money. I guess her parents gave up on her.

Yelling back and forth, they were claiming food that the house bought, and they were causing all kinds of ruckus. They ended up moving me into Detox Room 2 with G. I guess John had become a health threat with a fever caused by an infected tooth. G, my new roomie, was cool. He was a hard-working dude, in on, I think, crack. Pretty sure he will open up. All in all, though, a good guy that likes to talk s**t.

With the spooks on fleek, G and I said, screw it, and went to bed. For some reason, the A/C always kicks out and it got hotter than hell. Wasn't looking forward to the sauna sleep. Staff made a call and they reset the A/C. I guess it was on some Nest technology. We put on Netflix and my CBD kicked in. G told me not to snore, yet five minutes of TV and he's the one snoring.

I may have lost twenty pounds sweating. Holy hell! I woke up completely drenched. I opened the window, but across the way they have a lighted parking lot, so I kept the blinds shut. Unfortunately, not too much cool air made it in the room. It is still quite chilly in the mornings. I did my regular… Cup of yogurt, banana, and a bowl of Trix. I washed it down with some orange juice.

I went back to the detox house to brush my teeth and drop a deuce. Beings I was up early, all was pretty quiet. Life hack #137: Turn on sink full blast while rear is in full blast. Give it a flush and run! **NO TURNING BACK!!** One's got to find humor in life, regardless how tough the times can get.

I brushed my teeth and put on my deodorant and cologne. G was still zonked so I closed the door quietly behind me. I made my way to my sweet spot for drawing the picture of the day. The first thing that came to mind was the word, "STRENGTH," with a shield behind it. About this time, the morning squad came together. First Todd and Melvin, and before long Hobble Bobble (Charley) came out.

I made small talk with the smokers and decided not to partake in the outing for the day. I guess they said it was paddle boating on some nasty duck pond. Add that to 90-degree heat and a van with no A/C, packed full of people coming down off addictions… Mehhh… I'll pass on this one and take advantage of "blackout" detox phase, and completely social distance my ass.

I didn't realize, but I had quit alcohol, nicotine, and caffeine all at the same time. I was holding up pretty good, but I knew my anxieties were high and my nerves were on edge. I could see my ass going full panic attack, and I wasn't trying to do that. Some days were worse than others, but I told myself **NO TURNING BACK!**

As more people started moving it was medication time, and people fled to the nurse's door. I was in drawing mode, so I started another picture. This second one I traced a little bit, but shhhh… don't tell anybody. I drew up a king and ace of spades with the words, "Blackjack."

Before I knew it, the van was packed full and off they went. We did, however, have a couple of new faces that couldn't roll as well. Danny and Shelby came in from the east coast. Shelby was a pretty thing at 24, and Danny was 26. Danny looked like he done got his ass whooped or fell down a flight of stairs. I guess he was coming down off fentanyl, and Shelby dabbled in meth, but came in on alcohol before losing her wits.

Being empathic, I definitely needed some me time. I soak up too much bad vibes, and it starts throwing me for loops. In this alone time came these writings. In social distance style, I went to my bedroom and thought, why not document this journey? Hell, it would give me a reason to write a book when I got back home.

I decided to start with July 6th, 2020. Figured I would start the book exactly when I called Admissions and started this journey. The next thing you know, I'm twenty pages deep, and remembering all kinds of details. Interesting what the sober mind can do. Hell, half the time I couldn't remember what I did in the morning at noon time while drinking.

I took breaks here and there to grab snacks and some ice water. Before I knew it, the gang was back with In-N-Out Burger. This was new to me. It wasn't bad tasting, just more toppings than meat. I don't recall much of the next few hours, but what would you know? More food was being delivered. JoJo didn't cook on weekends, so they ordered out food.

I did get chest pains and a killer headache today. It seems to be re-occurring around 3PM every day. Which I guess would be five o'clock somewhere… like 5PM in Iowa… A coincidence??? Maybe… Body was trying to tell me it wanted its drugs. I was experiencing the withdrawal symptoms of my addiction.

Supper tonight was a chicken parmesan pasta from Big Mama's & Papa's. The staff didn't lie when saying this food was fire. Damn good! I guess they have the best pizza in L.A., but I may not get to try that. This boy is getting fatter by the day. If you go hungry in this place, you got problems.

The anxiety and headache finally got to be too much for me to handle. They gave me two hydroxyzine and shortly after a clonidine for blood pressure. Taking these pills always got me leery. They did help, but I was definitely afraid of getting hooked onto something else. Didn't want to arrive an alcoholic and leave a pill popper.

After filling my belly and laughing my ass off with G to Mike Epps's new Netflix stand-up (a must-see), I drifted off to sleep around 6PM. G came back and tried waking me up for the UFC fights, but... that wasn't happening. I ended up sleeping until about 11PM. Not 100% sure, but I think this was when I talked to the doctor.

I explained my situation to him about high level anxiety and that I wasn't withdrawing too bad, coming off drinking. I expressed to him that in having high level anxiety that it sucked I was lied to about where I was going. I guess others have been having the same issue. Just so happens if you don't advocate for yourself, you get stuck where they put you. Makes things just a tad bit sketchy.

The doctor had complete empathy for my situation, and he said he would do all he could to make sure I was moved to Rise Up in Dana Point. This was a good feeling even though it to may have been a lie. I was allowed CBD, but the doctor wanted me to cut back from the 3000mg. Which I can understand, but with pain and anxiety, at the moment, it was doing its job.

I wanted to go to bed, but beings the meds and full belly led to a five-hour nap, I was ready to do something. I decided to go out under the lighted canopy and write some more on my journey. I was getting closer to the current date, which would be great, so I didn't have to try to remember everything. I wanted to be detail-oriented, but that was a struggle in trying to remember two days ago.

I'm not sure what time I called it a night, but during my writings I took time to bullsh*t with the night staff. Eventually, I decided to head for bed to see what tomorrow would bring. I ended the night with a prayer that my kiddos were safe, and to lay on their hearts that Dad is doing fine.

Believe it or not, we got the air turned on, and I actually slept quite well for sleeping away five hours before bedtime. Better believe it… I had a yogurt and a banana for breakfast. This time I decided to wash it down with ice cream and an ice water. Figure I need to switch things up from time to time. I went back and brushed my teeth and then grabbed my drawing pad.

The drawing today, which I knew I was going to the beach with the group, was Carpe Diem… Seize the Day! Sometimes I get caught up in my writing and forget to make the best of my surroundings. As usual, the morning squad rolled out and there was a new gal. I think her name was Karen. Not quite sure what she is on but GOT DANG!! That's all I got to say about that. We're talking a walking-zombie-that-could-fall-asleep-standing-up mode.

After my art session, it was time for meds and a healthy s**t. So far, so good on that and no binding up. I have been eating a lot, but JoJo actually cooks pretty healthy. I then made my way to the girls' side cabana. Talk somehow went from a normal conversation to cussing and blah-blah, I don't know. I got up and started throwing some bags on the cornhole boards to get some early sun, and distance myself from the crazy.

(And then at this moment, all hell broke loose.) Not that Cheyenne would be one to bring drama, but this woman was on a mission.

"You can't hold me here… F**k you! I'm leaving… Where's my stuff? I know somebody that's best friends with someone that do this s**t, and if my insurance doesn't cover this, I will dispose you! (She meant "expose.") Better f**king believe it!"

She frantically paced back and forth from the staff office to the girls' house. All the rest of us were ready to hit the beach, and this crazy chick has everything held up. Who would have guessed, here comes her best friend of one day, pink-haired Kristin. Drama over-load with a couple of entitled drug addicts.

They finally got her to leave as she wanted, and then she got pissed they were kicking her out and she had nowhere to go. Can't have your cake and eat it, too, my lady. Then again, probably hard to eat with no teeth… but I did overhear them say they were going to mail her false ones. Interesting morning, that's for damn sure. Hopefully, this isn't a recurring thing.

In staying back once again, I went back to writing in my bedroom once the van left. I was getting a killer headache, so I took frequent short breaks. Like usual, these people can't do s**t for themselves, and the staff half-asses most of their work as well. One thing my parents and grandfather raised me to do was a good job, and to go above and beyond.

I threw away all the trash and cleaned up the kitchen before taking on life chores with Hobble Bobble. I thought she was headed to the beach, but I guess now she was my buddy for the day. Oh, woe is me!!!

Meds must be doing their job, though, with her. She is still bat-crap kooky, but she seems to be coming around physically. I talked with the male nurse (MoMo) on morning shift; he seems to be pretty chill and seems to have my back. He told me he felt sorry for me, and that the rehab system was totally jank. He said I was in good hands, and I was stable minded to ensure a promising recovery.

Momo told me to watch once one leaves the compound, how it triggers people to jump on board and want to leave. He said at West Hollywood rehab they lost a full roster of clients in a week. He wasn't lying… G had his wife visit and he was on board to leave, but they convinced him to stay until Friday. Charley wanted to go home, and Kristin was living on planet hell. Dude was defi-nitely right! It is a chain reaction, but not this guy. **NO TURNING BACK!!!**

I decided to do my good deed for the day and help Charley clean her sandals. I pulled off an old mechanic's trick on them. I used the juice from one of the hybrid orange/lemons off our fruit trees and some sugar. What would you know, they looked brand new. Beings Cheyenne's little fiasco delaying the beach trip, I decided to scrounge up some food.

I had my Mama on my heart when I saw mayo, relish, and tuna. Going to make me a tuna melt… Shoot! No bread. Back to the girls' house, and guess who had some bread… Charise. I grabbed two pieces off her and some cheese slices, and I then headed back to the guys' house kitchen. I whipped up a mean tuna melt with Doritos and some pickle slices. I was even nice enough to give Charley a taste, and she actually thought it was delicious. Mama would have been proud of me.

Of course, 4PM rolls around and the anxiety starts to hit me. I didn't do the hydroxyzine today, just the blood pressure medicine. What would you know…food? No, it was Joe's sponsor and his friend. The guys seemed pretty cool. The rest of the sun-burnt crowd waited on whatever JoJo ordered for the night, and Popeye's Chicken was on the menu.

After supper I sat down with Melvin and Aaron. We had a good life talk about our journeys, and how some of the people are entitled little beings broken by the system, with no respect for anything. I guess Aaron leaves tomorrow so the best to him on his sobriety journey.

Aaron was a hard-working dude from Washington that was in for alcohol. He was quiet but opened up to me before he left. He seemed like he was out of place, but sometimes that needs to happen to create the change we seek. I'm always rooting for Melvin. He keeps to himself, but he has a powerful voice, and you can tell he is woke. He spits truth but also listens to understand people.

Next thing you know, Todd is ready to play some Euchre. We had to teach Angie and John, but they caught on… well, John caught on quick. Angie, slowly but surely, figured it out, but her game play was cute. I think the younger crowd is realizing that the older crowd doesn't want to put up with their shenanigans and disrespectful behavior.

Edward (the staff member who picked me up from the airport) ended up taking my spot at the card table. It was all good, though, because it was fun to teach the game, have fun, laugh, and be sober. I'm not sure I had ever played Euchre while not drinking. I guess most any social activities I always included drinking... to have "FUN."

Not to forget being caught up to the current day before I hit the hay. I got to call Amanda today. This counselor, Stefany, is already making stuff up, and the manager is trying to tell me I know nothing, and that I was never supposed to go to Rise Up. I know Amanda will pursue these people, and hopefully the doctor as well, but who knows? The more I talk to people, this addiction rehabilitation is a corrupt money monster. In all reality, it's pretty disturbing and disgusting.

I told Amanda I was doing well and asked if she could reach out to the family and let them know as well. She said she planned to do her attack on these idiots tomorrow. I told her I would call her Tuesday to see what kind of hell she raised with these Admissions people. I'm learning to let go and let God. Taking the time to focus on my recovery, and not try to control things outside of my abilities. I finished my journal entry and called it a night.

Jimmy, the Poet, came through tonight for our last meeting. A cool gent that is active in his recovery. He ended up doing a cool creative writing exercise, and this is how mine went...

Creative Writing Project 1

Looking at my family as I face leaving them and headed through airport security... Emotions high; the hugs were poured on from all directions. Something I will never forget is my father hugging me. He told me I was more of a man than he would ever be because I reached out for help. I had reached a breaking point, and I wasn't content with the man I had become.

A leap of faith stemmed from a call to an admissions office. Seeing my kids one last time before hopping a flight to California for an unknown time frame. I remember hugging my son dearly and telling him to stay safe, and not worry because I would be back soon and be better than I was. Still not understanding that my vulnerability actually showed great strength. Not just to my family, but to my co-workers and friends. I was being 110% authentic with myself.

What I saw as failure was actually a steppingstone to ignite my life, in directions only the Lord knows I am capable of. Life will remain a struggle, but no struggle I will face will be overlooked. In moving forward, I will have to stay vulnerable and have the courage to face my demons head on. No more numbing the pain and suffering with booze but embracing the moments and seeing life for what it is, with a positive outlook.

Things started off a little different this morning. G was awake before me, for starters. I guess you could say I slept well. We had run out of yogurt, so I just had bowl of Trix and a banana. I'm not real sure but guessing that groceries will be brought in sometime today. Last night ended calm with no hysteria, so let's see what today brings.

As I came out of the bathroom I was greeted by a new face. It was an older fellow named Rob, who was a tech. I guess he had been on vacation. It seemed odd at first that he knew my name already but made sense when I found out he was staff. He seemed like a kind soul. Side note… My shoes were smelling pretty funky. I figured today I should make my laundry day. To my luck, the washer wasn't being used. I threw in my clothes and went back and grabbed my doodle pad.

As I sat searching for meaning in a new drawing, Melvin sat down at the table. He asked if I could draw him a logo for a business idea he had thought up. I politely took up his offer. He asked if I could come up with concept art for, "Knowledge Brothers, Inc." It was a podcast he wanted to start.

For some unknown reason, I already had an arc drawn on my page. I thanked God for the inspiration of an idea brought to life, and I decided to run with the line I had drawn. The Lord works in mysterious ways. You definitely have to have your receptors ready at all times, so you don't miss the blessings put in your life.

As I was drawing up the design for Melvin, he explained his idea of what the podcast would be. He explained in knowledge being power, that through his struggles he could provide help to the less fortunate. Every now and then, he would stop to critique my drawing, but he would say, "Nah, man, you good… Just keep doing you."

I mentioned to Melvin that knowledge is power, but health is wealth, and that living in pain, both physical and mental, and numbing it every day sucks. He agreed in that you can't apply knowledge if you can't apply yourself. Around this time, Aaron rolled up. He was counting down the minutes until departure. Today is his last day, and tomorrow at 7:45AM, he's headed home to Washington. Good, hard-working dude and I hope for him the best in his future endeavors and sobriety.

It was that time of the morning for meds to be administered. I grabbed my vitamins and for the most part, I was doing pretty well. From time to time, I would get head and body aches, but the anxiety was starting to subside. I would get lightheaded at times, but I did stop alcohol, nicotine, and caffeine, all as of 7-8-20 and there was **NO TURNING BACK!**

(Side note: Somehow Amanda knew I had a psych evaluation before I did... hmmm???)

Our first group meeting at 9:30AM was based on humility. It got really emotional really quick in the group. We started by coining out Aaron, plus he obtained his 30-day sobriety chip. Everyone got to say some words followed by a group hug and send-off. I know I have been saying it was Aaron's last day, but they kept on changing his plane ticket and postponing his departure home. Pretty sure this time they were following through with it.

Then there was a passage shared, and the tears started flowing. I think once it really sinks in, I might cause flash flooding in Los Angeles with all the tears I will cry. Todd, at 58 years old, shared some words and had the whole room in tears. He broke down in tears and choked up in his speech. Embarrassed and ashamed to be back a third time, but he proudly stated, "This time... I'm doing it for me!"

When we all gathered ourselves and wiped away our tears, we continued sharing. I, personally, have been having a hard time not choking up when I speak. Already an emotional sh*t show, and it's really hard to open up in front of everyone and show that kind of vulnerability.

I actually leaned towards vulnerability in losing the person I am supposed to be, because I had moved in with negativity. A man who was fun-loving and started a nonprofit to help people; that I couldn't find the strength to leave my own home. Group ended and we said the Serenity Prayer. I promise, Mama... I will learn the Serenity Prayer before I come home.

What a good start to a Monday, and what would you know, when I walked in the boys' house... JoJo was whipping up something better than the fast food weekend we just endured. Odd to think I would actually be excited for healthy, clean eating. Just ate breakfast and I'm hungry already again. I made mention to him about the fruit and veggie trays we made and that they never got put out. Although we patients are all a little messed up in the head, we definitely don't like seeing good food go to waste.

I had a meeting with Stefany and found out about a conference call with Rise Up in a few hours. The Boss must have been making ground with these idiots. I came downstairs to a group session led by Edward. During the session I came to realization that I am exactly where God wants me. Tom said it states in the Big Book that God places you where you are supposed to be, not where you want to be. This hit me pretty hard. I guess I was just looking for why I was lied to. I didn't need the luxury rehabilitation. It was supposed to be raw and real.

For lunch we had a fresh salad with salami and pepperoni, peppers, mozzarella, and that homemade ranch we whipped up last week. Sooooo good!!! After lunch, I did my first assessment, and then met with Stefany again. I guess that in this business, my arrival being two days out, that my bed was given to someone in need. The manager guy at Rise Up apologized for the inconvenience. I guess everyone but Amber and I knew I had been redirected. Kind of fishy, but I got the apology and decided this was home.

We then called Amanda, and I told her I was staying. She understood my viewpoint and told me she was proud of me. I mean, did I really see myself fitting in with some uptown rich folk? Hell, nah! We may be messed up here, but they are my kind of people. In ending the phone call, I told Amanda I would be calling the kids Tuesday, and Mom Wednesday for her birthday.

Once again, I came downstairs in the middle of a meeting. It was another group with Edward. This time I caught the end of it, but we talked about purpose and finding meaning in life; along with this in finding happiness. I was definitely soul searching. It was nice to finally get an apology. I left the meeting and went to the staff office. I told Morgan and Sammy that we cleared things up and that I was staying.

I told them I had no hard feelings for either of them. I related it to buying a $10,000 Van Gogh painting and getting a scribbled picture by a three-year-old. Morgan asked what he could do to make my stay better. I requested a 70" TV and a sleep number bed. He smiled and said he wished he could. I said I would be fine and that I would suffice with what was present. I'm where God wants me and there is **NO TURNING BACK!**

Conversation moved to the fire pit cabana area. One thing that stood out was… Well, Pink Hair (Kristin) and Bunny Lady (Nancy) decided to just up and leave the place. Thank you, Lord, on that one… Kristin was a handful, for damn sure. Back to talk… Cory, a quiet, gay dude in his early twenties, enlightened me about body brokering in depth. These admissions people are paying these 18–25-year-olds big money to come in for two weeks, rob their parents' insurance, then get them to leave and relapse to start it all over.

What a vicious cycle and absolutely sickening to hear about. I was broken by life and the decisions I made. The system is breaking 18-25-year-old kids to make these sleazeballs some fast cash. They don't care about people, or their addictions, and destroying the next generation. We are just now seeing its damage… sooooo messed up… poor human lives. Scared me in having teenagers.

I came back to the house to jot down what had happened during the day. I had been staying on top of my blood pressure. This last time it was 129/73. All I can say is CBD works, people.

Speaking on that, I need to talk to Sammy about getting more. Sammy is the Amazon Prime hook-up. I need CBD and some flip-flops. After catching up on writing to some YouTube tunes, I made my way to the next group session.

It was "A Fighting Chance," with Chad. He was a pro MMA fighter out of the Inglewood, California area. He did a workout with shadowboxing. We ended up moving some stuff and did the workout routine outside, due to COVID crap shutting down Cali to phase 1 again. Hell, I will be lucky to leave this state when my time comes with the way that things are going…

Hold this dang election already. This runny nose virus is getting old and taking its toll on people. Despite being outside in the hot sun, it was a really fun class, and hell, I needed a fighting chance right now. I definitely got my sweat on, but it was nice to release some toxins out of the body. I will, for sure, be looking forward to this group session in the future.

JoJo brought the heat for suppertime. Steak and mashed potatoes with a bomb-ass gravy. He paired it with grilled squash and zucchini and a tasty brownie. He definitely makes, "**NO TURNING BACK!**" a hell of a lot easier on a man. It's just going to suck when he doesn't come back to Iowa with me. I know I better get to working out or I will gain fifty pounds easy.

After supper, I did a little writing, and afterwards, Todd, Angie, John and I played some more Euchre. I didn't really know the game Spades, so I left that to the staff. We then had our last group of the day. We coined out Angie to Phase 2. I looked at who would all be leaving and told the squad when I coined out, I wanted a Zoom meeting. They would all be gone, and all the new people wouldn't really know my story.

We came back and finished our Euchre game. In running out of time, I told Angie I would draw her a picture incorporating the words, "Grateful for You." I pulled it off right at 10PM, while trying to mash a bowl of ice cream. Staff let me take it to her even though there weren't supposed to be guys in the girls' house after 10PM. She absolutely loved it.

I ended the night talking with Robby. The drugs were finally wearing off and he was catching the feels. You can tell the kid never had any guidance, and now he was a victim of drug addiction. I truly hope this kid finds it in himself to get clean or it will probably end in an obituary. They found him overdosed on the side of a road and he was even lucky to be alive right now.

<u>7 – 14 – 20: (Tuesday)</u>: *Talk with Kiddos:*

I woke up pretty stiff at 4:45AM from the shadowboxing routine. My alcoholic ass was out of shape, big time. I went to the guys' house for a quick breakfast, and to catch Aaron before he took off for his plane flight home. Sending prayers for a safe flight home and an awesome homecoming. Keep your head up, my man.

I went back to bed for an hour before waking up to draw with the coffee crew. I got the night staff dude to print me off a 3D black widow spider. Robby had asked me to come up with a tattoo idea for him. He asked if I would draw one with a skull on the ass; as the heroin spider with the words, "Deadly Bite." It actually came out pretty sweet. I will have to figure out how to add all the pictures I drew to the book I write on the journals.

During drawing I made conversation with Rob and Melvin. Then, of course, Charley rolled up. Coronavirus and the state shutdown, so talk naturally gravitated there. Not anything out of the norm, but Charley went bat sh*t crazy on the matter. Lately, this is just seeming more normal. Maybe it's the whole noodle brain thing they speak about in alcoholism.

She seems to be gaining some weight and getting around a lot better, though. Now the mind has just escaped. I saw that Robby popped out, so I escaped the madness to show him his drawing. He loved it; that's three drawings for three people down now. It's therapeutic in its own sense. It keeps my mind and hands busy, and it seems to keep me pretty calm and collected in my thoughts.

I then met up with Sammy. I got my Venmo account set up so I could do some shopping. I bought Adidas slides and some more CBD gummies. I then went to Nursing for my daily vitamins. For some reason, they had me at 300mg when I was taking 3000mg before bed. I had switched to 1500mg at noon and bedtime to help with midday anxiety (what the jar says…not per gummy).

For some reason, this wasn't good to them anymore and they

reached out to the doctor. I told them I want to keep away from popping pills. Yet for some reason, they were trying to push less CBD and more pills for my pain and anxiety. I did get them to settle on 1500mg a day. Not sure if I will split it up or just take it before bed. I think it was the package I had my 3000mg gummies in that screwed me. It was a 300mg little sample Ziploc baggie I got with my big jar. Is what it is, I guess.

First group session was with Rob. He read a piece about addiction and self-worth as an "inside job." That we start looking better on the outside once we escape the drugs, but sobriety, self-worth, and happiness are an inside job. Our physical appearance can tend to trick us. I mentioned that society will paint a picture of the perfect life on social media, when in reality, people and their families are all sorts of messed-up.

I knew this personally with the married life. Online we appeared as the All-American family that couples wanted to be like. There was a lot of past luggage, and a broken relationship filled with anger and hate. Anyone can smile pretty for a picture. I told my story of carrying the past with us in life.

"As kids, we have issues and put them in a gym bag. We hit our twenties and still got the issues from our adolescent years. The gym bag is full, so we start filling a carry-on bag. Then we get married and have children and guess what? We have that gym bag, have filled up the carry-on, and start filling the big suitcase.

I did this and got to the point I had all three bags full, and I mentally and physically broke after my divorce. I never dealt with the old luggage I was carrying, and I just kept on adding more to the pile. It was as if when I got on the plane, God was telling me to drop the luggage and come home. That I could stop carrying the weight of the world and focus on my wellbeing."

Now here I sat in a group session at a detox center in Hollywood, California. I was trying to find clarity and get straight with the Lord. It seemed like everyone in the group understood my take on this subject, and they found they could relate to it. I never really took the time to realize I wasn't letting go of the past. I was just carrying it on my shoulders.

After the meeting, I came out and met the new guy who came in last night late. Max (AKA: The Model). No homo, but this has to be the best-looking guy I have ever met in my life. Wavy dark hair, cut muscle structure, tattoos, starry eyes, and that Cali vibe. Nonetheless, he was a pretty chill and cool guy. I came to find out he was actually here two and a half years ago. He got straight and opened up a sober living house.

I guess life caught up with him and he fell off the wagon. The guy was very educated in the program. Said he knew the relapse was coming far before it happened. He said that he started isolating himself and got away from the program. I guess his drug of choice was some Oxy drug, and when he came in, he was also jacked up on fentanyl. He stated he was in on a sponsorship because of no insurance, but he knew the owners and management.

Ahhhhh, hell!!! Workout with Edwen, the super flamboyant head nurse. No hate, this dude owns being a diva. Dude was previously a professional ballet dancer in New York, and it showed during stretches. It went from yoga to kill-your-core in a matter of minutes and ended with free weights. It totally kicked my butt, but it was the workout routine I needed for my back. I went and sat in a chair in the sun to relax and bring the heart rate down, and to start working on this farmer tan.

LUNCH TIME! Bring it on, JoJo! He prepared a kale salad with grilled chicken, bacon, feta cheese, and damn... I can't remember. I took my food to the guys' house and talked with JoJo while he cleaned up. Such a well-versed cook with an awesome culinary background in the kitchen and it definitely shows. I will eat anything this man puts in front of me without hesitation.

After lunch, it was another group session, and this one was a hypnosis class. It was a proper British-speaking lady named Myrto. M-Y-R-T-O, mirror-toe, as she introduced herself. She was an alcoholic with 15 years sobriety. New people shared their stories, and when old man Todd started talking, all hell broke loose.

We were outside, due to coronavirus guideline crap. All of a sudden, police helicopters started circling our compound super low, and a big-ass military chopper came through. Crazy s**t! It was like a scene from the video game Grand Theft Auto. Los Angeles is no joke. Luckily, no criminals ended up climbing over our walls, and we headed inside for the hypnosis part of Myrto's group.

Todd was having a bad day, for whatever reason. The bunny lady ended up coming back. I guess they didn't make it a block from the detox house, and they were offered a bunch of hard drugs. Kind of messed-up and makes one think. People must work for the big insurance companies. It's amazing the things that I have seen and heard with the system breaking people to pad their pockets. It's an absolute s**t show, and very easy to be taken advantage of.

I guess Bunny Lady ended up getting all sorts of messed-up in her short time away. Pink Hair ended up taking all her belongings and got her all messed up on drugs. Then more or less left her for dead. It wasn't long before she was hauled off in an ambulance. Staff made up pretty quick with her belongings and had animal control people come get her bunnies. I guess the best of luck to you, my lady.

As we came back, I saw all the patio furniture boxes. I asked Morgan, the manager, if he minded if I put them together. He said that would be awesome, and Todd was quick to offer his help as well. I told Ty he wasn't in my book yet when he asked, but that today was his lucky day.

This Cali-vibing creature in white tights with black shorts, skateboarder shoes, a cut-off shirt, and backwards hat comes out to where we were working. He puts some classic rock on a small Bluetooth speaker. Kudos to you, Ty. This was the perfect mind shift that Todd needed for the day.

In getting my sweat on, we built a table and four chairs. I

almost lost track of the time and realized I needed to call my kiddos. Luckily, my son answered my call on the first go-round. I told them about the day, and how we had JoJo as our cook. My son had started detasseling and Madison didn't say a whole lot. They know I am safe, and I know they are safe. I told them I would be in touch. I told them I loved them and to stay safe as the call ended. Tears filled my eyes but... **NO TURNING BACK**!

Suppertime! JoJo brought the heat once again. Pan-seared salmon, garlic butter rice, grilled asparagus, and some blueberry bread dessert. I inhaled two plates and went snail mode. I know I can't bring this man home with me so I'll be damned if I don't try to eat as much as I can. I snuck away to start my writing for the day. I started to just jot down random things that happened during the day.

I had some Kid Ink streaming on YouTube. G came in, "Oh, snap! You get down like that!"

"Yeah," I replied. "I'm well-versed."

He came back with, "Looking at ya, I would have never guessed that bro!"

Just because we are some goofy-ass country people doesn't mean we don't get down in Iowa. We then headed to the last meeting of the day at the girls' house. Todd's sponsor, Mike P., came through to speak with us. He is a really cool guy with an even more amazing story. Everyone in the group got involved but Charley. She just randomly blurted out comments from the conversation before.

I also met a dude named Jimmy. He too was a chill person that challenged me to read the Big Book. I was informed that the office had pocket-size books of the first 164 pages. Edward informed me he would hook me up with one sometime soon. It was nice meeting the guys and hearing their stories. I definitely looked forward to seeing the guys again.

After the meeting, we got two new people in. It was a couple from Mississippi. The man's name was Kris, and his lady friend's name was Katrina. They seemed to be laid-back people. I'm going to guess, in for alcohol. I ended the night writing and chilling with the peeps at our new table under the lighted cabana. Tomorrow is Mama's birthday; hopefully, I can catch her for a call. Ty ended up hooking me up with a meeting with Cheryl.

Edward asked if he could read my journaling. He ended up really liking what I had started, and he then gave me some awesome insights on writing. I found out he, too, was into writing and actually going to school for it. Who would you know rolls up? Hobble Bobble, mumbling some gibberish that had everyone discombobulated, and then she walked off. Edward and I laughed about adding it to the writing...

And then, back she came... She bends over at the knees and goes into her psychobabble in calling the spirits. Edward asked, "Are you okay, Charley?"

She replied with, "Ummmm... Yeah... Ya know... my neck really hurts."

Love you, Charley, but damn, girl! You are definitely on a different playing field. She looked all over like someone was spying on her before she turned and threw her hands up and walked off. With that, I wrapped up my writings and called it a night. See what tomorrow brings for this newly sober man.

F irst and foremost, Happy Birthday, Mother! Hope you have a
great day. Second, damn you, Edwen! Rolling out of bed is
rough this morning. It was a good freight-trained feeling, and
there was no one to blame but my damn self. They say health is
wealth and I need to restore mine. Way too young to feel as old as
I do most days. Guess it only makes sense in consuming nothing
but alcohol and doing as little as possible for the last year.

I switched up breakfast and went with the double double. Two
bananas and two granola bars. It was then back to the new table
that Todd and I put together. The drawing time of the morning.
I'm not sure why I drew the mash-up picture that I did, but it
ended up turning out pretty cool. Been working on my shading
techniques, but I will definitely need an eraser because I have worn
down the one on this pencil.

While I was finishing the drawing, Sammy came out to smoke.
Corona talk came up, in that if we would be doing outings still. It
seems like it is mask up, and no one wants to shut down again
because of the financial damage incurred the first round. I stated it
was sad we live in a world where you can't go to church, but the
liquor store is still open. Sammy more than agreed with me, and
she stated it was sad to see it this way.

Group with Rob ended up being a short one today. It was
about acceptance of the defeat of alcohol. It struck home in my
situation because…

*"Hey, Alcohol! Yeah, you! F**ker! I surrender! You've won! I'm
done with you!* **NO TURNING BACK!** *I will surround myself now
with the tools to conquer you!"*

I did a little reminiscing after Group was over while I caught
some sunrays. The ol' body needed some vitamin D, for damn
sure. I got to thinking of all the fun times I had while drinking,
and in them how they accomplished nothing but a memory to
laugh about. As for the bad… Heck, where would I even start? I

can enlighten y'all later on some of the stupid things I pulled off. Just hold on for now and try to keep with my journey.

While in a state of suntan meditation, Charley proved her mental stability once again. Believe me... I couldn't make this s**t up if I tried. She asks me a question, I start responding, and she interrupts me to tell me to keep my thoughts to myself. I tried to get across that I was merely responding to her question. She then informed me that I was interfering with her thoughts and that I needed to learn how to shut up... Well... I'll just leave that one right there.

Excited or not, it was time for class two of the week with Edwen, and I guess tomorrow as well. Oyyyy, this unhealthy life! I just need to get past this health hell week. Just so happens that Edwen saw the drive in me and decided to push me. It sucks as of the moment but helps with my anxieties. Except the core... The core isn't digging what Daddy is doing right now. Too much neglect to this area, but with my back issues, it's definitely something I should be doing daily.

JoJo hit us with a twist for lunch today. Reubens, tater wedges, and a fresh garden salad. The thing was he didn't use sauerkraut or Thousand Island dressing. Instead, he prepared a homemade Russian dressing spread. While he cooked away, G and I worked on the ice machine. G has to always be screwing around with something. This guy will do whatever he can to get out of groups.

After lunch, I called Mama. I don't think she was expecting my call. She was hanging with her twin sister and their mom. I gave my mom a little insight about what was going on, but more or less just let her know I love her and wishing her a happy birthday. She seemed pretty stoked about the call.

It was outing time, and we all piled in the van. Rob gave me shotgun (thank you, sir). I may have complained a little about getting carsick and feeling claustrophobic... just saying. I don't do the whole packed-in-a-vehicle-like-sardines. Especially in the heat of summer with a terrible A/C system and everyone smoking. We ended up hitting Starbucks first, and my first thought was I don't do coffee. I ended up getting some peach tea lemonade and damn, was it refreshing.

So far so good in getting out of the compound and seeing the surroundings. From there we went to Griffith Park. It had an absolutely stunning overlook of Los Angeles and Hollywood. We were surrounded by mountainous terrain that one could hike, and the Hollywood sign in the backdrop. I got Rob to take pictures of me in front of the sign and the Griffith Observatory.

I had to get a history lesson from Rob. Small-town Iowa kid, I didn't know where the hell I was and if it was important or not. I guess the Griffith Observatory was in a bunch of movies, and it was a famous lookout point for astronomical folks. Some science guru s**t, but all in all, it was a pretty cool place. Off in the hazy distance, you see the new L.A. Rams stadium. It looked enormous from where we were at, and I could only imagine seeing it up close in person.

Never did I think that my poor decisions, addiction and allergy to alcohol, would have me in this exact location, but I soaked up every ounce of the here and now. It was absolutely stunning. Even though there were no floral aspects, there were green trees and bushes set perfectly in between hiking trails and deserty mountains.

It's quite the visual experience for a small-town Iowa boy that had only seen it in video games or a TV screen. It's all that and more for sure when you are standing smack dab in the center of it. The experience seemed surreal to me... How the hell did I end up overlooking the beauty of this big city? It was definitely a place I told myself I would bring my kids back to in the future.

When we got back, G was cleaning our patio area, and that's a "DO NOT ENTER" zone. I decided to go inside and do dishes. I miss you, Angie, but I'm keeping your spirit alive. If I didn't clean, I don't know if anyone would. Maybe staff, but that would be going out on a limb. JoJo snuck in behind me and started prepping dinner. We got to have a cool one-on-one talk about food and his life growing up. I could have talked to the guy for hours, but it was Group time.

Breath Work with Sam… I have heard a bunch of different takes on the class and remain undecided. I am, though, here to experience everything and find clarity in my life. To my luck, the class was an awesome experience. We did (Tom and I) two short breaths in and one long out for, like, five songs. We then slowed to normal breathing for four songs. My whole body was in euphoria and my feet were tingling. Sam said some people get emotional and will shed tears. In the slow breaths, I saw clarity in my life. That the journey wasn't over. It was like I crawled out of my failure self and into bliss. Tears started rolling down my cheeks. I didn't feel like I was crying in sadness, though. In bliss.

I tried breathing through my nose, but that was about impossible while crying and stuffed up. We took one last breath and opened our eyes. When we sat up, my exact words were, "Holy s**t balls… That was f**king different."

I am so glad I went and let myself go mentally to fully embrace what the group intended. Holotropic breath work is no joke (getting high off breathing). As I walked away lightheaded, I saw all the staff by the firepit cabana. Morgan asked how I liked the class, and I told him I really enjoyed it. Stefany then came up to me and showed me a text from Amanda. It was in gratitude of letting me call my mother for her birthday. I told her thank you and it was appreciated.

I started off on the wrong page with Stefany, but we are slowly gaining trust in one another. Hopefully, Amanda isn't getting too in-depth with her about things. To me, it would be completely biased and one-sided in how I was the problem, like she did nothing. I want to be honest with myself and don't want Stefany to have pre-assumptions of how or what needs to be changed before hearing my side.

As I walked back towards the detox house, I was met by Cheryl (the therapist.) We went back up to her office. She's not hard one to follow up stairs. A sundress or jeans... DAMN!!!! I will soak up this California scenery. When I first seen this woman, I could but only dream she would be my future wife. I was soon put in my place by someone informing me she was into women. Now this is my luck... and back to reality.

It was nice to finally sit down with her and get to talk and share my story. For some reason, she was under the impression that I had shared information about my past with Stefany. I told her this was completely wrong and that I had only spoke with her about Admissions and that I thought I was at the wrong place.

We ended our meeting with three things that I needed to dissect in my life. Impulse in an ADHD aspect, failure/defeat, and resentment of the past. She gave me an assignment of getting a sponsor to help me understand the twelve-step process. She told me in starting with a sponsor here in California, that when I went back home it would make for an easier transition back into "normal" life.

We did supper and I came back and wrote in my journal for the day. I put on a Cali-vibe playlist on YouTube while I did my writing. 311, Sublime, and Red Hot Chili Peppers were streaming, the good oldies alternative jams. Just when I thought there wasn't another group meeting, Ty had his own idea of a meeting.

We all gathered in the girls' house living room and watched the UFC fights. Well-played, Mr. Ty. My insurance will probably be billed $5,000 a day, and I'm being watched over by twenty-year-old kids that are just newly recovered. Watching UFC fights like it will somehow be beneficial to my recovery process. Hell, I don't even like watching TV. I ended up coming across a pocket-book of the AA Big Book. Cross that one off the list, and now to start reading it.

In a recap of meeting the new Mississippi folks, Katrina and Kris, it seems like they are settling in well. I found out through conversation that Kris's stepson was recently murdered over a dice game and flexing a BMW. Damn! Katrina seems pretty chill. She doesn't talk a whole lot but has already started in on helping with house chores. The two ended up partnering up and playing Spades against John and Ty.

<u>7 – 16 – 20: (Thursday)</u>: *Master Chef*

I finished off Wednesday trying to read my AA book. Just so happens that four people felt the need to sit by me, light the fire, and then start blabbing on about what had happened for the day. Here and there they would ask me a question, when it was obvious I was reading, and then try to apologize. I guess it is communal living so I can't get too upset.

It was Piss Test and Breathalyzer Day in the hood. Still negative and zeros, like the day I walked in. I thought maybe my CBD would leave traces, but it didn't. I went to grab my vitamins from the nurses, and I remembered to weigh myself... got to be kidding me! I was still 201 lbs. I haven't gained or lost a single pound all up in here. With JoJo's cooking, I am surprised I haven't gained twenty pounds.

It was Store Run Day. Still pisses me off that they give out cigarettes when ya piss. What about me being a non-smoker? I keep on asking for T-bones and ribeyes and they just laugh at me. On top of these people getting tied into human trafficking with body brokering, they also promote poor health decisions and penalize those who choose healthier living.

Charley was making a shopping list, and she said she would buy me pencils and erasers as a going away gift. Lately, she has been saying she is going home tomorrow for the last few days. Hopefully, she stays halfway sane upon returning home. She has a huge heart and great intentions, but it's just that she is... BAT S**T CRAZY. Anyways... next week I need to buy myself a hoodie. It is cold as shit in California in the mornings.

We came to find out that Danny and Shelby took off at 4AM, walking the streets. They got that taste of freedom when we did our outings. Danny seemed like he needed to sit put, but Shelby, on the other hand, was a looker and you could see rebellion in her eyes. I remember seeing she wasn't afraid to flaunt her stuff while brushing her teeth that one morning. Got dang! She had old G and me humming in our room. We are definitely going to miss that view in the morning.

We are now down to ten people when we were just full, like, four days ago. From what I am understanding, Danny even stole G's shoes after he had given both of them clothing when they came in. It never fails. There is always something happening, and this place could easily be a TV reality show. I guess we will see if they come back.

From what I was picking up on, I believe that Danny was on a scholarship from Shelby's parents' insurance, and their last day was tomorrow. I'm not quite sure how leaving one day early makes any sense. They sobered up and got some food in them. They got a free plane ride to Hollywood, and now back to partying it up. Hell, they were probably tied into that body brokering, the way they jetted.

For Fitness, we had an open session with Eddie. I steered clear of sit-ups. The core was a little tender after the last two days. I decided to focus on back and chest. At the end, I got Edwen to do a bicep burnout with me. Had to show him the guns weren't just for show. After the workout, I got a little sun and read another chapter from the AA book.

Before lunch, Cheryl and Niko strolled in. All I can say is God is good and he listens. The other day I mentioned to someone about therapy dogs. Yesterday Ty brought his new puppy, and today Niko brought in her therapy dog, Bergen, the Beagle, and Cheryl had her pet birds. Coincidence? I think not.

JoJo made a fresh lunch, as always. Buffalo chicken wraps in a spinach tortilla. I got him to hold back and save some food. He had been cooking for, like, 25 people and we were down to only, like, fifteen in the houses with everybody. I haven't had a bad or off-tasting meal from this guy.

Group with Cheryl was weird and hard to stay focused. One, because this woman is drop-dead gorgeous. Sitting there looking like Lara Croft from Tomb Raider. Olive green pants with a black tank top and her hair French braided. To top it off, her birds were crawling all over her head and pulling down her shirt. Not sure what I was learning, but my mind was definitely imagining, to say the least.

The brain was kind of drifting because I knew cooking with JoJo was up next. We were doing stir-fry bowls. I got to prep the meat. JoJo asked what kind of music, and I was quick to request James Brown. Let's just say we messed that kitchen up. That kitchen is my happy place.

I stripped out beef flanks and then JoJo let me cook it. He taught me how to do the pan flip you see on cooking shows. It took, like, maybe three good tries, and I was going Master Chef on that stuff. Pretty cool new life skill to pick up. I wish they did this cooking with JoJo every day. I know that I could have learned a ton from this man.

Starting to really miss Angela at the house. I ended up doing dishes by myself. I know Angela would have been there to help. G and I went back to the room and started a Chris Rock stand-up on Netflix before our next Zoom meeting.

The Zoom meeting more or less sucked. They do it in the living room of the girls' house and the internet is trash. I will add it on the C.R.A.S.H. report for tomorrow. I get to do them now that I am out of detox status. They need a better router and wi-fi boosters throughout the properties. They spend enough dumb money that they should be able to afford something to bring better internet.

Word on the street is we are getting a new girl tonight. Hopefully, she is peaceful like the Mississippi duo. It makes for a better recovery process. Charley may leave or something tomorrow. As of now, she has had the refrigerator door open in a boys' house for over an hour. Lord knows, and only him, what the hell she is up to.

7-17-2020: (Friday): Come and Go

Nacho slipped me my last full gummy. 3000mg meant I was out cold for the night. Beautiful sleep… I woke up at 6AM, and like normal, it was a little overcast and chilly until the sun burned off the clouds. JoJo said something yesterday that it probably won't rain until October. If it does, Lord… I will lay down in it and be washed by your water. I believe in your mysterious powers.

Guess a guy came in last night. Charley said it was an old Asian guy. Will see how true that holds to be. Especially in the fact the woman hasn't slept in like three days. She needs some horse tranquilizers or something. Her mind is completely disappearing. I guess it's the noodle brain that they speak about in advanced alcoholics. Stuff is 110% true. I ended up pulling off two drawings during coffee hours. One was Hawkeye-themed, and the other was a custom design for Melvin for a car detailing business idea he had.

JoJo did breakfast this morning. Scrambled eggs, sausage, fresh fruit, and French toast… absolutely stellar! I typically don't eat fresh fruit, but I went ham on some strawberries, mangos, and blackberries. Not sure if it was in cutting alcohol and needing carbs, or the fact I had quit chewing tobacco, too, and my taste buds are changing. Another good note is the back was finally feeling decent. Last night I was hurting good.

First group was led by Todd. It was about admitting surrender to the addiction and that we are powerless. Sammy joined and shared about quitting drinking at the age of 23, after a two-year binge after her first son's father died. Luckily, she didn't go to treatment. She just prayed to the Lord and found the strength to stop. Now, 16 years later, she still won't touch it, in being scared of its power over her.

Reminds me… Before first Group, I got to get filled in on G's history. His dad was a hustler and ran drugs. He was killed when

G was just nine years old. His mom disconnected and told his sister and him that she never wanted either of them. From, like, 12-13, he pretty much raised himself and started hustling the streets.

After first Group, I decided to get my daily sun and read my AA chapter. It seriously goes from 60 to 90 degrees in 30 minutes out here. It is crazy, and that sun is no joke out west. Hopefully this weekend, my fat, white butt can get some sun on the chest and back. By the time I finished Chapter Five, I was full of sweat, and it was time for next Group.

Group was with Stefany. Crazy enough, she, too, brought her dog. Ozzy, a mutt-looking dog, possibly a terrier and wire-haired mix. He was a super nice dog that made his way around to everyone in the room.

Group was odd, to say the least. Charley was climbing on couches and interrupting constantly. Trying to get light in the room when she had sunglasses on. Can't make this s**t up. Melvin got pissed as all hell. Steph would ask a question, then turn to texting on her phone. Not the most professional recovery atmosphere. We somehow managed to go a full hour, but the chemistry was completely off. The meeting just had a strange vibe. I couldn't even tell you what it was about.

JoJo did a crab cake with sweet corn and a fresh salad. Different, but still tasty. Breath work was next, and to be honest... I wasn't feeling it. A full stomach and trying to hyperventilate just doesn't go well. I went to it, anyways. The class is definitely relaxing, but this class was different from Wednesday. It wasn't the outer body feeling and tears. It may just be that I walked in with the wrong mindset. Sorry, Sam, for napping, I will be more present next week.

Met the new guy after breath work. Guy's name is Daniel, probably mid-twenties and he is in college for art. Charley was just a little off on her observation last night. Not quite an old Asian dude. I started a third drawing in down time before Group with Darrell. We talked on distractions that spur a relapse. Charley was on her antics again, and Darrell wasn't playing it. He called her out and she shut up. I think we all learned something good. Hey, Stefany… take notes from Darrell.

JoJo did a shepherd's pie for supper with a cheesecake dessert. Damn! It is like all we do is eat at this place. Hell, I think I'm still full from breakfast and have had lunch and supper, plus snacks. I did dishes after supper to go outside and find the new guy, Daniel, was already gone on his own will, and now we have a new girl. Petite blonde gal that looks early twenties. Guess we'll see if she comes out of her shell by the end of the night.

Which she did… Cheyanne from near Seattle, Washington. Pill popper that was all about opioids and smoking weed. She seems pretty chill with a sense of humor. This is her first time in rehab. I decided to call it a night. I popped my CBD gummies and put on "The Secret" on Netflix. Reminded me of my daughter as I drifted off to sleep. Madison and I would always binge-watch crazy shows on Netflix.

7-18-2020: (Saturday): Lake Balboa

Woke up at 5:15AM… not sure I will ever get past the time difference on my West Coast stay. I ate a small breakfast, and my drawing turned to shading practice. Cheyanne actually woke up early, as well as the others, too. Must have been a full moon or something.

I was feeling pretty sore, so I cleared the area, heading back to the workout house. I did some sprints, planks, push-ups, and dips. I finished with a lunge and some basketball dribbling for a little extra cardio. After exercise, I did some tanning and read Chapter Seven in the AA book. Over 100 pages in so far and I find the book very interesting.

We made small chat at the house, waiting to go to Lake Balboa. I decided to go this time, and I am glad I did. It was a very scenic drive to it. Mansions spread throughout the desert hills. Huge buildings all relating to the entertainment world. Crazy to be in the middle of all this, just soaking it in. I'm literally in the city where movies are made.

Lake Balboa was in a suburb called Encino. The park was really nice, and people were everywhere, regardless of the COVID crap. John and I did a swan paddle boat. A little fruity, but as we navigated the lake, we talked about our past drinking and our future sobriety. Thank God for dry heat, too. That sun was beating down on us.

When we got off the boat, two gals and some kids strolled up to go on the boats. Holy Lord, have mercy, for this gal's shorts. A butt so perfect, peeking out the bottom of a torn-style jean short. For a brief moment, I thought to become a stepdad all over again. **NO TURNING BACK!**

Ha-ha… God has definitely created some beautiful women.

We came back to the house. Should be chill the rest of the day. Ron, the weekend tech, ordered Papa John's pizza and wings for lunch. Tonight, Kris said he would run the grill. We got chicken,

burgers, and hotdogs. G's ol' lady swung through, and so did
Max's. That Max and his girl look straight out of a magazine.
Never seen two humans of this beauty.

Kris slayed it on the grill. Hobble Bobble was up to her regular
shenanigans. Playing around in the fridge for, like, an hour and
throwing away all kinds of good food she said was bad. Then cut
up stuff to put on the grill and never grilled it. Ended up being an
early night, and with everyone's stomachs full, we parted ways.

I know my daughter is writing me, and I think Mama is, too. I
was going to wait to write them when I had received their letters,
but I may write them earlier. Probably finish off the night reading
my AA book. I'm slacking on praying, but I have God in my heart.
I really need to seek spirituality. That and figuring out this sponsor
thing. Jimmy is supposed to roll through on Tuesday, and I plan to
ask him that night after the meeting.

7-19-2020: (Sunday): Beach Day

It was the normal morning, conversing with Todd and Melvin. The night shift techs, Kanika and TJ, joined in for the convo. I started a peacock drawing as a tattoo concept for Kanika. I will probably end up keeping what I draw and color a copy for her. She wants a rainbow color scheme throughout the feathers.

I did another workout on my own. I figured out a way to do biceps. There was a dolly that weighed about 40 pounds. It wasn't in the best shape but worked for what I needed. I ended up doing a deep squat with it in hand and hit twenty curls. After getting the heart rate up, I switched over to the morning tan and read. Today's read was Chapter Eight, "To the Wives." Won't lie, the read hit deep.

Before heading to the beach, I whipped up breakfast. Three eggs, peppers, cherry tomatoes, ham, and red onion. Making people jealous that walked through the kitchen. After breakfast, I did dishes for my chore for the day. This Iowa time difference... got all this done before most people even woke up. I guess I was choosing not to be heavily sedated as well. Some people here are getting knocked out to receive sleep.

So, we all piled in the big white van and headed for Santa Monica. It was crazy, we went from 90 degrees and no clouds to 70 degrees and overcast. Beach was pretty desolate but looked nice. Cody, Melvin, and John took off walking, and Todd, Max, and I found a spot to camp on the beach.

It was chilly for sure with sun-kissed skin. Todd took off to piss, and Max and I conversed. Before you know it, with almost the snap of fingers the clouds disappeared, and the sun came beaming down strong. The beach completely transformed in a matter of minutes. The water became of a bright blue, and let's just say ladies galore came out wearing next to nothing. Now we're talking California vibes to this Iowa boy.

Cody and Melvin headed back to the van. John ended up

meeting up with Todd, Max, and me. Todd and John ended up going out in the water. All that I know is this water aint the gulf, for damn sure. That water was bitterly cold. It reminded me of jumping in a trout stream as a kid with my brother. We met back up at the van and somehow lost Kris and Katrina (the Mississippi duo).

Max and I decided to take off walking and see if we could find them. Sucks, you get out here and people just take off and no one has a cell phone, so no way of contacting anyone. At this moment is when "Hollywood" became a nickname for Max.

Come to find out the guy did model, and for four different agencies. The kid has a pretty cool background. It's crazy to think his super-hot girlfriend, who is also a model, is not the best-looking girl he has been with but that she is "Cool." He told me that he only dated actresses or models.

Just taking this scenery all in… I look up to see some high-rise apartments on a hillside. No sh*t… I've seen these buildings on Pornhub… just saying. Max told me they cost over $15k a month just to rent, and that I was probably right on my guess.

Good ol' Hollywood! Max told me porn was everywhere. Almost make you sick. Said innocent girls come out to a saturated market to start their acting careers and get shot down. In despair of chasing a dream, they get offered money to do porn and so the story goes. He said most end up homeless on the street, addicted to drugs.

We finally found Kris and Katrina. They ended up walking past the bathrooms that were close and ended up walking like a half mile to the next ones. They ended up walking almost all the way to the pier. We piled back in the big white van and headed for Veggie Grill. It was a fast food vegetarian menu that Max picked. It only cost like $200, so hopefully, it tastes good.

We arrived home, kissed by the Cali sun. I was burnt to a crisp. I will need to even this tan out next week. Veggie Grill was decent, but not worth the money and hype. About an hour later, pizza showed up. I drew some colored pictures with Cheyanne at the new table. You can tell she is young, but she is pretty chill so far. Guess they are deciding to do a 7 PM meeting… see what that is all about.

Max ended up having his girl, Kat, over again, and damn, is she ever so easy on the eyes. Maybe she has friends that dig farmer-tanned, chubby white guys. I can only dream… If so, the kids may be upset that dad isn't coming home. Ha ha, **NO TURNING BACK!** Guess I will let Max miss the 7PM meeting this one time.

Before Group, I was able to touch base with my sister. Bless her heart, she deep cleaned my entire apartment. She shampooed the carpets, did laundry, you name it, and it was done. Seems like everything is kosher back home. I told her to let the kids know I would be reaching out to them Tuesday to touch base.

Group was at 7PM and didn't start till 7:30PM. Think they got talking to Max or something. They were both from sober living homes, and Max being an owner of one, seems to know a lot of people. Group was cool with C.J., Nick, and Chris. Got some good insight on working the steps once I get back home. Guess it was worth the wait and shows that I'm not in control of anything.

Ended off the night writing and finishing up some pictures. Got an idea for tomorrow's drawing for Charley. Guess she is headed home tomorrow and doesn't even know it. Hopefully, no layovers or hub flights or the poor gal won't make it home. Signing off for now… Goodnight!

Kind of strange but woke up at dang near 7AM. G's words were, "Homie, you were snoring loud as S**T!" Beings I woke up late, I just ate a bowl of cereal, and then I started on Charley's jukebox picture. Cheyanne took the colored pencils last night, so the picture stayed black and white. I thought the drawing from my dome came out pretty cool. I can replicate something I see, but I have a hard time drawing from the dome.

JoJo was in the house for breakfast this morning. He was doing fried eggs, ham, hashbrowns, and fresh fruit. While he was doing his thing in the kitchen, I read Chapter Nine from the big book and got my dose of vitamin D. Not that I really needed it after the beach, but what the hell. One key thing I have noticed is my taste buds have definitely changed. I'm eating damn near everything put in front of me and it's delicious.

First group with Rob was a coining out party. Coining out is getting a coin of completion when you go on to the next stage of recovery. At this facility there were three phases. Detox was Phase 1 and 21-30 days. Phase 2 was still monitored but more freedom, and Phase 3 was sober living, where you had freedom but still had to take piss tests and had a curfew.

Melvin, John, and Cody are all starting the next step of their sobriety journey. Melvin and John are joining Angie at the Phase 2 house. I'm sure Joe can't wait to be reunited with Angie. Cody is headed to Max's gig called Venture to do sober living. They all seem focused on their journeys, and I wish them the best in conquering their sober lives.

After the meeting, which got emotional but stayed positive and straight-forward, I grabbed my contact list to get numbers. Next thing ya know, G strolls in with Morgan and his new shoes. I forgot to mention mine, so tomorrow will be Amazon shopping with Shameca. I will end up buying a hoodie as well for these chilly mornings. The more sun-kissed my skin gets, the chillier it is at night and in the morning.

Second Group was with Edward. It was a two-minute silence exercise. I actually escaped my mind to try to understand my purpose. I watched a tree move in the wind. What was its purpose on Earth? Shade, aesthetics, oxygen... what about myself? I let my mind escape to an open world. When I shared, John said he wished he could shut down his brain and be in the moment like I did. I guess in **NO TURNING BACK** it is living in the moment and accepting/embracing life and moving forward.

I also brought up perspective with the chat I had with my son at the river by my parents' house. To me, watching the water flow by with nature's sounds and the sun setting was most tranquil. It let me escape the worries of the world for that moment in time. To a fifteen-year-old, though, he saw adventure. Boating, fishing, jet skis, and quads. Neither of us was wrong, and I told him I understood both sides. He actually agreed with me, though. He said just chilling with his dad in nature was calming.

Group ended and JoJo brought on chicken pesto sandwiches. They were freaking delicious. So light but refreshing. After lunch, I missed group to speak with Stefany. She brought Ozzy again. The dog is a cute little guy. During our talk, I opened up to her about life. I think it surprised her about my depth as a person and what I went through. Also, that I knew exactly how I was destroying myself.

I totally missed Group and walked into Fighting Chance, with Chad, the MMA dude. It was nice to get a good sweat on. We all wished him the best before he left. His wife was dilated to a 3 while we were doing the workout. Prayers, my friend, to a healthy delivery to Mama and the new baby.

JoJo pulled through with shrimp fajitas for supper. He had churros for a side... Damn!... I was in heaven. I talked a little more with Max, and his life doesn't ever seem not to amaze me. Dude asked if I knew what Bumble was. I may be small-town

Iowa, but, yeah, I know what it is. He told me he was ranked in the top 6 hottest guys in Los Angeles area.

Dude has only been with top tier women, his dad was a pro football player, he is hands down the best-looking male I have ever seen, and partying with the stars, but the kid almost overdosed and killed himself because he feels empty, and now just trying to save his pride. It's humbling as a small-town guy, thinking what it must be like living it up in Hollywood, and this guy will tell you every horror story after the cool wears off in the first month. Great girl, great job, and still couldn't get past his demons.

After supper, I hooked up with G and Todd to make apple crisp. G was packing tonight, too. I guess he leaves tomorrow. From what I know, Edward took off to bring another new girl back, and I thought I heard something about another guy tomorrow. It is a never-ending revolving door in these rehabilitation centers.

7-21-20: (Tuesday): Got a Sponsor

S ome reason, I woke up at 2:30AM. I thought it was closer to 5AM. I got dressed and went out to draw like usual. When I realized the time, C.J. asked if I wanted to play some Nintendo Switch. I won't lie, the thing is pretty badass. Charley ended up coming over. I swear this woman never sleeps. And then, G popped out. They all ended up going back to bed, and I played one more game of Overwatch on the Switch. Grateful he let this old-time gamer on for some games.

I headed back to sleep, and I ended up sleeping in till after 7AM. I don't really remember what I ate for breakfast, but I drew a tribal sun and colored it in with colored pencils that I got from the new girl, Sara. I tried getting vitamins before first Group with Rob, but Max must have been chatting Gwen's ear off.

I talked to Sara, the new gal, for a bit, and I found out she had some things happen. Admissions painted some elaborate picture, and she ended up here at Mariposa. She was super pissed. I told her I was in the same boat two weeks ago. Sucks being lied to when we are so far away from home and family.

I headed to first Group, and we started coining out G. This guy did everything in his power to avoid meetings, but he was always doing some kind of chore or job for the compound. At 55, the dude acted like he was in his mid-twenties, and he was physically fit, too. Hope the guy the best, and that he follows through with coming back to work for the detox center.

The topic of discussion was the gift of sobriety. It was cool hearing everybody. Kris has been pretty vocal, but Katrina and Cheyanne started coming out of their shells. Rob finally got fed up with Cheyanne blurting out randomly, and he kindly made gestures as to shut up unless directed to speak. She is young, though, and I guess it's better than not participating.

Wasn't but enough time to change clothes and it was time for "Fitness with Edwen." I was so ready for stretching out, minus the much-needed core. That diva makes it look sooooo easy. By the time stretching is done, my fat butt is in full sweat, but it's getting easier with being more flexible. My back has really only caused problems for, like, one day. I finished with an upper body dumb-bell workout. Then again, they don't have pressure fronts like Iowa.

JoJo… my man!! Steak, sweet potato fries, and a cold broccoli salad with cashews, cranberries, and cherry tomatoes. Absolutely delicious! The steak was super tender, juicy, and seasoned perfectly. After lunch, we came to find out that Sara packed up shop, and she was headed for West Hollywood Detox. From what the employees say, it is nicer, but the staff and regiment absolutely suck. But… best wishes to her on her recovery process.

After lunch, Myrto, M-Y-R-T-O, stopped in for hypnosis. I must have not understood correctly last time. She sounds like she is British, but she says she's Greek. I love when she cusses, too. This proper little lady with a potty mouth. Last week, she was all about masks, but today she went mask off during first half, and California was back to stage 1. Politics and the media have the people of America all screwed up. Scared today… but not tomorrow.

After hypnosis, which I need a new topic for next week, JoJo had pre-cooked supper. Chicken over noodles with a garlic lemon pepper sauce and sauteed green beans. I skipped on the water-melon. I still can't eat that nasty fruit, for some reason. With my belly full, I tried reading the last chapter in my AA book, but my eyelids became heavy, and I started drifting off. I pocketed the book, and I took a nap.

I was woken by Todd trying to figure out where I was. I pulled the book out again and finished the eleventh chapter. Jimmy, the Poet rolled in, and we did a creative writing. Jimmy did like a ten-minute freestyle poem; dude can spit. After the session, I asked Jimmy about sponsoring me and he said he would. Just so happened I would be his first sponsee. Cross that off the list… first 164 pages of AA book read and got a sponsor.

Creative Writing Project 2

Feel > Think > Do > Be > Say

Topic: Mr. Brickman – Fill-in manager at Job

Q1) How do I feel

Pissed, angry, worthless, belittled, tired, anxious, scared, targeted

Q2) Why do I feel this way

This man is a boss, not a leader. He demeans people and takes zero accountability of workplace failure. His actions have crippled employees, and the culture in general. It's to a point where he is saving face over ass. He had the nerve to tell me I was taking the company to Hell, when it was him and the old HR manager hag.

Q3) Is it rational/ do I have the right to feel this way?

As a union rep and also a human, I would say yes. I don't just fight for myself, but for my coworkers' rights. We are humans and this man is pure evil in flesh. They break people to control them, and then act like they helped you. He should retire, but his greed seems to drive his ego and controlling demeanor.

Q4) What am I going to do to change it?

First and foremost, I am changing myself to attack problems with a clearer mind. What happens in darkness will be brought to light. I need to Let Go and Let God. Focus on me, and what I can change. Having empathy for situations and applying what tools I have to help.

A new guy came in tonight and I was moved to the boys' house, and finally out of the detox house. I got moved to a huge room and all by myself. Although a lot nicer, it was hotter than shit up there. We had the detox house at like 68 degrees. I will make do, though, **NO TURNING BACK!** The new guy is from Chicago and his name is Joel. He had been in treatment and came off relapse. The guy seems pretty chill. Should stay awhile, but it's hard saying in these times.

Closing notes of the day... Totally forgot that I did my Amazon shopping with Shameca. Got me a cool hoodie and some cheap, but interesting-looking shoes. Hopefully, the shoes fit. They only had whole sizes and no half sizes. After that, I called my son. He quit detasseling but is still helping his uncle. My daughter didn't really say much. She was too busy playing Plants vs. Zombies. Heck, so busy she never wrote my letter. Guess I will have to send one first. Happy they are safe and healthy, from what I know.

New room did me well. That, or CBD and watching "The Last Dance" put me to sleep. I'm not sure I even moved in the bed. Just so happens my new room windows face the sunrise. I woke up at 6AM and headed out for my morning doodle session. On the way out, I started my laundry.

Not sure why Spider-man came to mind, but it is what I drew. Ever since Cheyanne broke the pencil sharpener, I have just been bummed about drawing. I can't get my crisp lines. Tomorrow is the store run day, so I should be able to get one. Waiting on first Group, I made up breakfast. Leftover steak, Mexican rice, eggs, red onion, cherry tomatoes, sweet peppers, and some hot sauce. Won't lie… I'm quite the chef. Look out, JoJo… just kidding.

But, of course, Charley joined Rob and me. Still going bat s**t crazy. I mumbled to myself and was informed to shut up. The woman aint got much to lose up there. One hour later, she is asking for hugs and help and crying about who knows what. Most of the people and staff just try to avoid confrontation with her in general.

First Group with Rob was a short one. With people in detox, we only had four-and-a-half in the group. The half being Hobble Bobble. You never know if her mind or body is going to be present or gone. The topic was "last place we used." Easy enough for me.

I had a 12 pack at my apartment with my kids present. I drank nine and my parents showed up. I split the last three with my mom and dad. We hit a Mexican joint and, of course, one margarita wasn't enough. Dad helped me finish the second jumbo. We came back home, and I chugged water the rest of the night.

Rob's story was a bit more out there and thank God for another chance. The dude de-constructed a razor and slit his neck and wrists. He went thru his jugular, and somehow didn't bleed out and die. Said it was the most driving factor to never be in that spot again, and I believe it… God is Good!

Morning time was cold and overcast so it threw off my tan-and-read time. Off schedule, but I kept in mind that I would still read it. It was back to Edwen's dungeon. Before open gym, I talked with Edwen. He is supposed to bring his guitar tomorrow. I got a good pump in. I worked shoulders, abs, and biceps. Also did some lunges and ball slams. After getting a good sweat on, JoJo had a delicious Cobb salad prepared.

With a full belly, we hit the road. It was Starbucks and a road trip by the new Rams stadium, but traffic said otherwise. Six minutes into traffic, it turned chaotic. We turned around and did some downtown sightseeing. It was still nice to get out and do some sightseeing outside the compound. The compound's walls start to wear on a guy.

When we got back, I tried to get ahold of IH Mississippi Valley Credit Union about short-term disability on my truck payments. I ended up just paying the damn bill. Before Breath Work, I met with Stefany, aka Snowflake. Just my luck, my son didn't answer. I went to Breath Work hoping for spirituality presence. I ended up falling asleep. Every time my mind got close to escape, I would detach and lose my breath in sequence.

After Breath Work, the sun was perfect for tanning, so I got my AA book out and I read, "The Doctor's Opinion," as requested by Jimmy, the Poet. I have completed the book, and I am ready to engage in step work. I also tanned and read Chapter Five again. Hoping to get more of a tan before hitting the beach again. You burn fast out there as a chubby Iowa boy.

JoJo whipped up meatloaf and new taters for supper. Hell, I even ate roasted cauliflower, broccoli, and carrots. After supper, I tried calling Jimmy, but he didn't answer, and it turned into phone tag. I'm not too worried. I will try again tomorrow.

Time was moving slow, so I decided to write my daughter since she is too busy to write me. While writing her, my Adidas slides were delivered. Merry Christmas to me! I can't wait for my hoodie tomorrow. I went upstairs to write in my journal and found myself back outside.

I stopped by the nurse's office for CBD. Pretty sure she was hitting on me. Told me I looked good, and that was actually nice to hear, for once. I can always find a way to make her laugh. I told her she was going to start teaching hip hop classes. She said I would break my ankles, and she was probably right. She was actually a trained hip hop dancer before ballet dancing.

I finished off the night writing in my journal. I ended up writing my prologue. I wanted Edward to read it, but he is out picking up a new guy as I write. Speaking of new people… Joel said he will probably be gone in a few days. Then Cheyanne was on a rage, throwing all kinds of fits. Guess she was "cheeking" her meds and then taking them in masses to simulate a high. She had been isolating, with a sunk-in face, and acting all sorts of weird. I guess we'll see what happens. She was all about packing her stuff up and leaving this joint. As for me… **NO TURNING BACK!**

C an't say I slept the best. I woke up multiple times throughout the night, like I was going to miss something. As I headed to bed last night, they brought in a new guy named Chaz. For some reason, I ate like a horse for breakfast. I had an apple with cinnamon and sugar, a banana, three eggs, and two toast.

After breakfast, I tried helping George (maintenance tech) put together a swing that Sammy ordered. Just so happened they boxed two of the same tapered pieces, so we couldn't even complete Step One. First Group was with George on how we were doing. George related with me in saying he, too, was half-assing being a father. Distracting our kids so we could selfishly indulge in our addictions.

Edwen forgot the guitar, and I let him know how much it broke my heart. Guess now he is promising to bring it Monday. I will put it on the C.R.A.S.H. report as a reminder for him. We ended up doing a core circuit for Edwen's fitness class. All I know is these exercise routines get me grunting and cussing like crazy.

JoJo served up a spinach with strawberries, blueberries, goat cheese, and walnut, with balsamic vinaigrette. Super tasty, my friend. I ended up eating two heaping plates. Might as well stay eating like a cow for the rest of the day. I reached out to Jimmy after lunch. He put me on the Lord and asked me to be of service to others. Thankful for a great dad, I was already on top of this one. What can I say, it's in my nature.

Niko did Cheryl's group after lunch. It was her first time hosting one. Guess Cheryl was feeling a bit sick. The group was more or less another checkup. It was cool. The new guy, Chaz, came. He is 36 with an eight-year-old. He is from South Carolina. His story was straight out of the AA book. It was definitely proving of him being powerless over alcohol.

Sammy checked and let me know my Amazon things were

coming. After the meeting, I met up with Edward and let him read my prologue. He gave me good insight on how to tweak it to read better. He said he really liked what I wrote, though. I then called Amanda. I filled her in on things and did what I could to line up talking with the kids tomorrow afternoon.

Today was cooking with JoJo. Knowing this definitely gets me hyped up for the day. I got put on homemade mac & cheese. It was interesting. For the cheese sauce, he added egg. He baked the mac 'n' cheese, and the egg became a binder for the noodles. Altogether, we had ribs, mac 'n' cheese, grilled asparagus, and a peach cobbler. Still managed to go cow mode.

Cow mode definitely caught up with me. In trying not to regurgitate, I slipped away for a nap. I then came down and did after-dinner dishes. My hoodie and shoes arrived, and both fit well. Happy camper on that note. Dick (tech) thought I was journal writing and asked if he was in the book yet... So here is Dick, ten months sober. He is a younger guy that is cool but has a gambling problem, but I didn't tell ya. He is claiming he wants royalties when this becomes a New York Times bestseller.

I spent the rest of the night writing letters to my family and Amanda. Something got into me, and I felt the need to just connect on an intimate level with the people in my life right now. The new guy rolled in about 10PM. Travis, he is a tweaker of sorts that seems pretty lit as of the moment.

Had a good sleep last night. Woke up at about 6AM to another gloomy day. Typically, it gets sunny and melts off the clouds. I guess some coastal aspect, or something came in and it's staying chilly till like 11AM. I ate a small breakfast and did a badass Indian boy drawing. I got quite a few compliments and actually surprised myself.

First Group was with Ty. He had come in for day shift. I guess he was headed camping for the weekend. Our topic of discussion was "Helping Others." Most all of us were people who enjoyed helping others. I related with Kris a lot. Help people every day, but no one ever asks us how we are doing. When we do need help, they are nowhere to be found… "That mother f***er!" We said it at the same time.

JoJo forgot he had to do breakfast, so everyone was on free-for-all mode. I went back to my room and did a short workout to some Sevendust on YouTube. Edwen is gone till Tuesday, so I got to stay limber on my own.

Can't take Edwen home with me… even though he would probably join… but got to do things on my own.

Second Group was with Snowflake. Still not fully getting this chick. I'm getting this resting bitch faced, super liberal, she-is-superior vibe. There is compassion or something there, just zero empathy. I can't quite put a finger on it. Slowly, she is seeing who I am, so hopefully, we can come to terms. She is always blurting out, "I get it! I get it!" It's just not welcoming or understanding. I feel a lot of the others get the same vibe by reading their facial cues in Group.

I had to call the kids' mother to get consent to do a group session with the kids. JoJo brought over a fried chicken sandwich and homemade coleslaw. This man never ceases to amaze me with the dishes he brings to the table.

After slamming lunch, we did Breath Work. I had Katrina put

it on C.R.A.S.H. report. It's hard filling the belly, and then trying not to fall asleep in a meditation class. I'm still yet to have that experience from the first time, and that sucks because it was awesome. For some reason, I just can't hone back in.

Straight from there, we went into Group with Darrell. I left group at 4PM to do a session with Stefany and the kiddos. She was surprised with what they said and how they viewed me. They want me happy. I hid my fears from them so they wouldn't stress.

After supper, I found out I had received a letter from my sister. Odd she sent me envelopes the same day I sent off letters. I think she wrote before I called because most of the letter was stuff I talked to her about on the phone. Speaking of letters... what I sent out... Stefany said it wasn't a good idea. She didn't know they were already sent... Whoops!

We did a group with Niko and Gregg. They both had cool stories. They both had been feeling down. They needed to get in a group atmosphere and help and receive help from others. It stayed pretty chill, and all the new people came.

I finished off the night doing my journal and shooting the sh*t with the residents. Got Nacho laughing with my dance moves. Told her next year I was headed for *America's Got Talent*. I got to talk with Travis, the "new guy." He is 21, from Indiana, and has two kids. He is in for opioids/painkillers/meth. Seems like a cool dude, just off on the wrong foot early in fatherhood and life. He actually came out and said I was a genuine dude and that he had respect for me. That was a pretty cool way to end the day. This next writing was one that came to me today.

"The Hero"

There are heroes everywhere. Young, old, tall, small; real life super-heroes. The funny thing is when a hero is present, they seldom know they are one. The hero, many times, is shattered and torn. They are tired physically and emotionally, and depressed or filled with anxiety. The hero had a bad day at work/school or just lost a loved one. The hero is human. The hero sheds blood and cascades tears.

Don't get me wrong, though; the hero can be a joyful child, sick in health, stricken by cancer, but dancing gracefully with loved ones, showing no fear of an ending life. To a 100-year-old WWII vet taking his last breaths from a hospice bed. They are everywhere, in every shape and form. The homeless man who shares his spare change or splits the burger he was given with a man of the same nature, not knowing when he would eat again. He has empathy and knows broke and hungry.

The heroes are out there, and in most times, their work is done, not even knowing they are impacting someone's life. They are just being authentic with themselves. Whether it's of self-servitude or showing courage when the weight of the world is crushing them, physically or mentally. They somehow find a way to address the chaos with faith, hope, love, strength, courage, and compassion.

Brothers, sisters, neighbors, parents, friends, public officials, the famous, to sons and daughter,s and the list goes on. The hero can be you. Yes, you! When you feel a failure and broken down, just remember, sometime, somewhere, you were someone's hero. Not knowingly, you changed someone's life or inspired someone. You were or are their strength, courage, faith, hope, and love. **YOU** *are a* **HERO***!*

Remember, Jeffrey, let go and let God. You are exactly where you are supposed to be. Trust in the process, and **NO TURNING BACK!**

7-25-2020: (Saturday): Booty Mountain

I can't believe it… Nearing 100 pages since conception, and I have started my second composition book. I guess I will see where Book 2 takes me on this recovery adventure. With a sober mind, and a mission based off **NO TURNING BACK!** Let's just see what living in the moment will bring.

I woke up a little after 6AM. Todd must have been in the hot seat because he became my theme for morning doodles. The drawing actually turned out pretty good. For some reason, Cheyanne was up and wired. She doesn't seem to shut up, and on top of that is a compulsive liar. But we're all messed up, so I guess, roll with the punches.

We had a cleaning crew come in. Two Mexican dudes. The main dude's name was Oscar. While they cleaned the kitchen, I did my little weekend workout routine. Always feels good to get a sweat on.

I made small talk with Oscar when I was done exercising. Came to find out he was a recovering alcoholic. He gave me kind words, and said if I kept my mind busy, I would nail my sobriety. He told me he had faith in my sobriety, in what he saw in me in that short time. Grateful for his words.

When Oscar and his guy went upstairs, I started on breakfast. I forgot the hash browns were the ones G messed up by thawing. I cooked up over medium eggs, some thick cut bacon, and hash browns with cheese. It actually turned out pretty good, and the residents ate it up. Some good ol' Iowa-style cooking with butter, Lawry's salt, and bacon grease.

After breakfast, we took off on an outing to Runyan Canyon. I guess the place is some famous exercise hike that YouTubers and famous people regularly hike. This small-town Iowa boy didn't have a clue what this place is. We parked at the bottom of a gigantic hill, not too far from the Magic Mountain Club. Guess that's a famous deal, too.

We were in a pretty uptown, upbeat place, for sure. What really sucked was the walk to the front gate. My legs were on fire, and we hadn't even started the hike. I started off with Todd and Max at the base of the hike, but before long, Max was gone on his own. Going up this path was no joke, but to locals it seemed rather easy.

The scenery... MY LORD! Thank you to the creator of yoga pants and crop tops. To hell with Lake Balboa, this place right here rocks. The main path winds back and forth, while you could see other trails that led to peaks of the rock formations. Todd and I stayed to the cement path until we got near the top.

We passed a little private residence, and the smell of reefer was strong. Let's just say that someone was feeling good. As we came around the corner, we followed a Kardashian-looking chick up a one-way, the wrong way. Big fake breasts and a huge, implanted backside... What dreams are made of. She ended up cutting up a closed path, so Todd and I carried on a bit further.

We didn't end up running into Max, so we decided to head back down. Going down this mountain was a dream with a breeze. It actually almost turned into a difficult walk because gravity had us stepping down pretty hard. We had to hold back from trotting. We stopped a couple times to take in the views of fancy homes set into the hills with the LA skyline in the backdrop.

The girls just kept on coming... My Lord! Not even sure where they were coming from behind us. Their clothes matched the weather. We ended up seeing Cheyanne hunched over a bench. Looked as if to be a washed-up pedestrian waiting to be eaten by vultures. Her addiction, malnutrition, and heat exhaustion had her all messed up. Plus, she wore all black.

The name Booty Mountain came to mind instead of Runyan Canyon. Hands down, one of the coolest things we have done. I can only hope we get to go back. The place wasn't really all that far from the compound. When we got back, all kinds of hell broke loose before Chinese came for lunch.

Cheyanne had heat exhaustion, and Travis stumbled out with

his shirt off. Guess he was power puking. He ended up being taken to the hospital. Guess that's the coming-down-off-meth phase. After lunch, I played Joel in bags, and I got beat four games in a row. I guess I need to practice. Tray came back and he seemed to be stabilized.

Still full from lunch and El Loco Pollo arrived at our compound. Barely anyone ate. It hit me to make homemade chicken noodle soup with the leftovers for tomorrow. Hopefully, JoJo has enough veggies in the fridge to pull it off. I had already saw that he had chicken bouillon in the cupboards.

After supper, I called Jimmy. He gave me another hiking destination called Branson Canyon. I guess, see if we can do an outing there next week. He is coming tomorrow to visit me. I guess it's kind of cool being his first sponsee. Not just helping me but strengthening his program as well.

Sammy and Justin seemed all pissed off, and the vibe at the house was definitely off. Stage 2 house came and took our grill for the night, and Todd was pissed because he had food prepped to grill. Looks like grilling tomorrow night instead.

Kat swung through to see Max... Damn, bro, hold on to this one... oooo-weeeee... Sammy ended up sending her home early. Guess Sammy stayed late because C.J. and Tray, the night techs, got in a confrontation. See what tomorrow brings of it.

My neck and head have been killing me. Not sure why. It may just be muscular, but in stopping drinking it hasn't gone away. I figure I will ice it tonight. It's more of an annoying feeling. Looking forward to tomorrow and the beach. More of God's fine creations. Let there be sun and buns once more. Nothing better than a Sunday thong parade. Hell, I think I'm going underwater tomorrow as well.

S econd day in a row I rolled out of bed, and I hit my knees and prayed. I went down, as usual, with my sketchbook. For some reason, I was drawing a blank. Then after three attempts and erasing it, I drew a picture of drawing a picture. Ended up coming out pretty cool. Some reason, Cheyanne's crazy ass had been up since 2:30AM. I guess she is becoming the new Charley. She also had the whole table covered in stuff, which was a total Charley move.

Since Phase 2 stole our grill last night, we had steak prepped in the fridge. Todd and I decide to do steak and eggs for breakfast. Ended up turning out pretty good, and we fed quite a few bodies. Now it would just be nice if someone helped with dishes, but control what I can, and I guess it keeps me busy, so I don't mind it.

We all kind of congregated around the new table and conversed while we waited to go to the beach. Seemed like it was going to be a hot day. The sun had been out and kicking since 6:30AM. Max leaves tomorrow and has been acting pretty weird. I wish the best for the dude. His relapse about killed him, so hopefully he stays working the program and steps. Would suck to hear he lost the battle.

We piled in the drug smugglers' van and off we went. Still love seeing the L.A. downtown as we hit the P.C.H. (Pacific Coast Highway). We were met by a series of supercars. The first one had a rainbow vinyl wrap. Money got money on the beach front. The sun never popped out today, for some reason… well, it was the fog off the water. It was cold and overcast and I just wasn't feeling it today.

Before we took off, I put my crafting skills to work and embraced my inner teenager. Hand-crafted a big ol' schlong out of sand. Chaz added to the detail with some black seaweed that he found. Made for some great detail. Glad that teamwork could make the dream work. Beings it was a public beach, I erased it with the kick of my right foot.

Justin ended up taking some weird back way home. It was cool seeing some different scenery. We went thru Koreatown. Kind of reminded me of Chicago style separation. When we got home, I threw on homemade chicken noodle soup and tuna melts. Spoiling these folks with my cooking, but I enjoy doing it. Like usual, I ended up doing dishes again. Almost like déjà vu.

Think Charley done did lost it for good. Now she upsized to a huge beach bag. She is walking around talking to herself. I guess she is letting everyone know that she is going to the beach. I just don't know what to do about her. Hell, I don't think anyone knows what to do with her. Some think they are misdiagnosing, knowing she will relapse and be right back. It's crazy to think it, but this field is definitely run by insurance malpractice. She has great insurance, and they will absorb every last dollar.

Guess we are losing three people tomorrow. Max, Joel, and Wesley. Wesley was shy at first, but he ended up opening up a little bit. He was an older black gent that was from the Bronx. Steel worker by trade that had been in California for five years. Guess he started smoking meth back in January.

Joel is headed back to sober living. Guess he went on a binge. He lied about starting up a business as a subcontractor and got the $10k COVID loan. He went high roller, bought an old BMW, and rented out some penthouse, and then got all messed up on drugs. He came to Mariposa for a blackout period before heading back to sober living. I told him to be careful and that the government would be after him for that money. He seemed too naïve to care. As for Max, I guess his scholarship is up.

It was phone call time, so I decided to reach out to the parents. Mom and Pops were definitely glad to hear from me. Twelve more days and I should be homebound. That is, in that the Lord doesn't have different plans for me. Missing the kiddos, though, and could use their hugs.

After the call, I teamed up with Edward (Team Shamrocks) for some Spades, and we spanked Max and Katrina. Then we turned around and smoked Max and Ty. Beginner's luck, I guess. It was my first two actual full games of playing the game of Spades with a deck of cards, and not on some old computer.

Ol' Miss (Kris) ended up grilling again. I think the majority of us were still full from lunch. We have, like, nine people, and it seems they still order for eighteen. During supper, Jimmy, the Poet stopped by. I enlightened him on my story, and we went over "The Doctor's Opinion." It was cool dissecting the words and bringing more meaning to the book.

Beings I am leaving in twelve days, Jimmy wants to push things and try to get through the fourth step. I'm all for it, and sure I can revisit things with an Iowa sponsor at AA groups. When Jimmy left, I met with the group for a guy named Sam, talking for H&I. Cool dude with an awesome story. Kid had two-and-a-half years of sobriety. Went from eating out of trash cans to teaching at UCLA, and he also acquired a Bachelor's degree and Master's.

I'm still battling this neck and head pain. Be nice to get home to a chiropractor. I am doing it sober, though, and **NO TURNING BACK**. Probably as bad as it is because instead of getting it fixed, I just numbed it daily with alcohol. I know it's got a cure; it's just holding on a while longer. See what Edwen can do for it. It really doesn't seem to bother me sleeping, so that is a good thing.

I ended up in a talk with Max and Ty. It started out with wondering how taxes work on OnlyFans. Guess Ty and his ol' lady decided to join the page. This coronavirus got people doing whatever they can for money. This world is going crazy.

Then Ty brought up the 10k COVID loan... same one that Joel scammed. Knowing what I know... You may think you slid by and then two years later, when you're doing good... BAM!!! Garnish your wages and leave ya broke. So, yeah, screw all that scamming the COVID loan stuff.

I came to journal for the day, and Ty busts out with a bunch of candy. They had it for the last four hours. Peanut M&M's, Sour

Patch Kids, and Reese's Peanut Butter Cups. Not that my fat ass needed any candy, but I did indulge my fair share. About the same time, Edward rolled in with a new guy.

New dude was from Seattle, WA area, and his name is James. He was in on a meth addiction that had been going on for six years and he lost control. His heritage is of the Pacific Islanders. Dude seems pretty cool, and he said he likes the vibe of the place. Seems like a good-hearted, hardworking guy that took the wrong path… kind of just like myself. For now, adios, world, and let us see what Monday has in store.

H ad a bad dream throughout the night and woke up around 3AM. It was odd because I don't remember it, and I fell directly back to sleep. JoJo was coming in to cook so I just had a banana and a Pop-Tart to tide me over. My picture for the morning was an ashtray and cigarette smoldering away, with a "NO SMOKING" sign in the background.

It was a definite Monday, and a case of the "F**K-ITS." Todd was pissed, but he did the same thing when Angie, John, Melvin, and Cody took off all together. Hopefully, it just comes and passes, like last time. It's like he gets pissed that he is still stuck at Mariposa.

Morgan and Stefany were anxiety-struck due to being short-staffed. JoJo showed up late for breakfast, and you could tell he wasn't too concerned about being at work. Must have partied a little too hard over the weekend. Guess the dude likes to do his clubbing. Personally, I was feeling some pain, but all right emotionally, until Charley and Cheyanne started in on their antics.

Charley had half the table filled with her belongings. Papers, notebooks, breakfast she won't eat, some flowers she picked, markers, colored pencils, and two drinks. It's beyond ridiculous, and the staff hasn't been saying anything.

As for Cheyanne, she just lies about everything, and interrupts or doesn't shut up about irrelevant topics… Supposedly she paid off ten thousand dollars in fines for her brother getting caught stealing a six pack of Mike's Hard Lemonade… Like, come on, Cheyanne. My daughter of thirteen is more mature than you and makes more sense when lying.

Lord, please forgive me! It is more of a rant. I'm trying to stay calm, but it affects the quality of meetings for us that are trying to stay straight. JoJo made blueberry pancakes, scrambled eggs, and bacon. I started reading a new book about a guy who was a drug addict that recovered through a Buddhist mindset. It's a book about spiritual awakening and that's exactly what I need.

After breakfast, we did a small coin out session for Max leaving. Kid has a lot going for him. Pray he works the steps and keeps out of his own head. After the meeting, I made a point to vocalize/rant about house concerns to Morgan. It was a kind of a six of one, half dozen of the other. She will be gone in a few days, and we are sorry.

Our process group was with Snowflake. I'm still not vibing with this chick. She seems disconnected from the group and conversations because of her cell phone. When she is connected, it seems blunt and extremely biased. She tries being compassionate, but it comes across almost naïve and sheltered when it comes to family issues. Then again, she doesn't have kids, so how does she relate with the stresses?

Lunch was chicken Caesar wraps, and I heated up some leftover chicken noodle soup. Joel found out he has to stay another day, and this guy aint having it. The new guy, James, has been sleeping all day. Guess he was all ramped up on meth, and I found out that's typical in coming down to sleep for days. Think he had been up for a week before he got here. Some old chap rolled up. Chains hanging from his neck, just chilling outside the nurse's office. He was instantly transferred to West Hollywood.

It seems to be more reoccurring that people are being led to believe that they are going to some beachfront mansion for recovery, and then they end up at this detox center in the ghetto. After lunch, I did a little meditation in my bedroom to some Shinedown music. I was interrupted to go on a Starbucks run with George. Beings we were short-staffed, we went for a cruise with George. No one was up for doing groups.

We drove up through Griffith Observatory area. I thought George was going to stop and take pictures, but he took a different road and drove through the park. We then shot over to the famous Hollywood Boulevard. Streets weren't all that packed, as usual, because of COVID regulations. Nonetheless, there were beautiful women out everywhere.

Max chuckled to me and said, "You haven't seen sh*t. These girls are maybe 5's, and some 7's. All the hot girls are in the Hills, day partying at mansions."

I believe the dude. His last girlfriend of five years was an aspiring actress. He said he used to party at the hilltop mansions. He stated that he didn't miss it, though. He said it was all-day-and-night chaos, fueled with free drugs and alcohol. I mean, not that it's a good idea… but at that age, I would have been partying like a rock star for sure. Maybe in my afterlife when I come back as Post Malone, Jr.

We drove past all the Hollywood stars on the Walk of Fame. Would have been cool to actually walk it and read them, but George said that was a no-go. We hit construction in the road, so we hung a left and hit Melrose Street, and headed back towards the compound.

On a little side street, we drove past where Jimmy Kimmel Live! was filmed. The area was the tourist trap of Hollywood. Didn't really get to see it in its actual life, beings hardly any life existed on the streets due to the Rona. Walking it with street performers would have been cool, but for this trip it was kind of bland.

We got back just in time for Fighting Chance, with Chad. Still no baby yet. His wife is still sitting at 3cm dilation. We had some newbies, started off with Chaz and Cheyanne lost. Odd that last Monday, Cheyanne was telling me I was doing it all wrong, yet today she could barely figure out the first stance. You got to remember she is always talking about beating people's ass or putting them in armbars at 73 pounds soaking wet. HA!

About halfway through, we lost Chaz and Cheyanne, and we picked up Travis. Guess he had done some kickboxing. Chad did a few more advanced combos for him and me. Travis actually ended up finishing out with me. You can tell the kid didn't have structure and was needing it in his life. He has the drive and shows he can be a respectable young man; it's just the drugs consumed him. Hopefully, he sticks with the program. He has a three-year-old and a seven-month-old.

After supper, we watched the Brandon Novak documentary. At age 15, he was the youngest pro skater, he starred in *Jackass and* wrote a Top 10 New York Times bestseller. He was a 3X millionaire that went to a small sack, filled with a few things that were his worldly possessions. He became addicted to drugs and alcohol and gave away all his fortunes. He is currently in long-term sobriety and has written four books, and he also works in the addiction rehab field.

After the documentary, I sat down with Ty and Joel. Joel is on some next level, not caring about life, but you can actually tell the guy, deep down, is good at heart. On top of falsifying information to get the $10k business loan, he is also filing for unemployment. Which I could only assume is illegal as well. Being covered by short-term disability and FMLA, one can't claim unemployment.

Maybe he will skate free. I just know, with my luck, that I won't ever be tampering with the federal government. Trying to get clean and have life going well, and then get nailed on that shit… enough to make a man relapse. That's one thing that isn't in the plan of **NO TURNING BACK**.

Joel took off and Ty was talking about an app his buddy and he were trying to create. It was going to be like Airbnb, but for sober living homes. Pretty cool concept and I hope it takes off for the kid. Like I said earlier, I don't even know if there is sober living in Iowa. Something I might want to check into, once home.

Ended the night in a deep conversation with Edward. We tend to go back and forth. I know he wants to get me to think in terms of how I handle things, but I reverse it to if he was there. The guy can get you on some next level thinking, for sure. He told me he was going to print off his book he wrote and bring it in for me. I headed for bed and set the TV to native sleep music with flutes.

Twenty days sober! Instead of drawing this morning, I grabbed my journal. The long talk with Edward left my entry a little short of finished last night. Guess the new guy dipped and was a no-show last night. Cheyanne showed up to the table, and talk moved to how the system and insurance works. Enlightened her that people are getting rich breaking 18–25-year-old people. She tried making her own sense of it, but I think she totally missed the point.

8:15AM rolled around, and that sun was right on time. I read my new book and got some vitamin D. That sun was powerful, so I called it quits a bit early. I came back to the new table and sat with Kris and Sammy. We conversed about the stimulus check dropping next week. I should be receiving another $1700. My mind was actually pondering doing Phase 2. Probably be another two weeks or so.

I won't lie… I want to see my kiddos, but work doesn't interest me in the least, and coming home to a bank account full of unearned cash and short sobriety doesn't add up. Not sure if my work screwed up on unemployment or the people here just don't care about screwing the federal government. I just know I'm not taking any chances, because my luck sucks.

I hosted first Group. George was gone with Katrina shopping. Topic turned to how the workplace has changed, and how the cultures have gone from family to self-centered. Big businesses don't care about their employees' wellbeing, and social media has everyone wrapped in everybody's business but their own.

I convinced Edwen to do an open gym after giving him crap for forgetting the guitar again. Best part is, as soon as he sees me, he goes into guilt mode. I had him set multiple alarms on his phone to help him remember. I did end up getting a great workout in. Worked over the whole body and did a double bicep burnout.

JoJo did chicken pitas for lunch. Light meal, but it was very refreshing. After lunch, we had hypnosis with Myrto, M-Y-R-T-O. I love how she always spells her name out in her little British accent. The new couch came in and Myrto was super psyched. I must have been a little full from lunch because I started snoring. Myrto gave me a little shake to bring me back to life.

After "Advanced Nap Time," the sun was perfect for an afternoon tanning session. Beings that I isolated for the last five years; my body was indulging on some sunshine. I found a spot over by the girls' house, flipped a towel out, and beached my ass like a whale. After crisping the skin, I bounced around a little bit before making my phone calls.

I tried putting all the pieces to the puzzle together, but this compound is all screwed up. There are a bunch of weird decisions being made. Guess Travis said he woke up to Joel jerking him off, but didn't bring it to anyone's attention at the time... Ummm ... If I wake up to a dude jerking me off, I'm throwing punches and blowing rape whistles. I'm sure as hell not going back to sleep in the same room.

I guess the story is that Travis was also making advances at Cheyanne. The dude has been sulking around all day and completely isolating. Hard to say what people will do when they are coming off the drugs, and what his family history was with sexual abuse.

There is a new older black dude from Massachusetts. His name is Cliff and for some reason he didn't have to detox, and they put him straight with Ol' Miss. Then somebody made the executive decision to put Joel with me. I wasn't really feeling this s**t... Hey, let's put the guy who is jerking people off in their sleep with Jeff. Maybe it's not true, but what the heck.

Joel had talked with Silicon Recovery reps, and they are keeping him at this house now until Friday. It hit 4:30PM, so I reached out to the kiddos for my phone call. My son answered, but he was fishing with his buddy, Carter, so I called Madison. She didn't answer, so I called their mom. Luckily, she answered, so I got to talk with Matte. I guess she is sick. Been throwing up, bubble guts, and a headache. Doctors saying it's a strand of the coronavirus … Come on, Election Day!

Told my daughter I may do Phase 2, depending on if the stimulus check drops. Said, "Heck, I may not even come home." She told me not to do that, and to at least come home for a month before taking off for good. I guess in letting God take the wheel, who knows what is in store for me next? In doing God's will, one must go where the Lord takes them.

Found out Todd is leaving for Phase 2 tomorrow, and Wesley is headed for a sober living facility for two weeks on some quarantine shit before heading to New York. Morgan somehow already knew I was considering Phase 2. I guess word spreads fast to everyone. Everyone but me… nothing new.

If the stimulus check doesn't drop, it's probably not feasible. I would run out of money and get behind on everything. That and the fact my short-term disability is still all jacked up, and it's not being direct deposited yet. I should have like five hundred dollars coming, but from where I stand, and no communication, it is definitely hard saying.

JoJo made a ziti bake for supper. It, once again, was absolutely phenomenal. This man is making it hard not to gain fifty pounds. After supper, Mike, Todd's sponsor, stopped in for the H&I panel. The guy's story reminds me of that Brandon Novak guy from the YouTube documentary. Mike's last rehab stint, he was, like, 6'4", 120lbs, beer in one hand, and a needle in the other arm. Now he is 220lbs and runs an insurance restoration business, and he is sitting good financially.

Toward the end of the meeting, Jimmy, the Poet came in. I apologized for missing to call him yesterday. We took a quick smoke break and came back to do creative writing. Our video inspiration was Brené Brown, on courage and vulnerability. Our writing exercise was about strength, weakness, goals, and fears. We finished the meeting with a short Eric Thomas video. This man is a phenomenal motivational speaker. This was my creative writing of the night.

Creative Writing Project 3

I am enough! I lost my way and, Lord, I want to come home. I found you sometime in my teenage years, but never took the time to get to know you or accept you in my life. Having kids at an early age with a beautiful young girl; we were kids trying to raise kids, and life managed to tear us apart. I tried with everything I thought possible at the time to hold our family together. It just didn't pan out. In trying to not feel like a failure, it was exactly how I felt inside as a new father.

I found that I was destroying myself physically and mentally. I was constantly in and out of homes with friends and family. I was breaking the law, and breaking relationships, both personal and work. I recall a time getting super s**t-faced, and then sleeping in a sliding door closet for two days. Part of me didn't want to be woke or found. Part of me hoped someone would find me. I finally woke and no one had come to my rescue. It was you, Lord, that took care of me in this time and yet I still didn't accept you.

I started a construction job, and my foreman was a recovering heroin addict. He was an angry soul when I first met him. The second day on a job, I hugged him and put on Christian music which was referred by another employee. From that day forward, we started a brotherhood. He actually got me to try a church in Tipton, Iowa.

The first time I went, I liked the church, and when they did their acceptance prayer, I didn't raise my hand. The next time I went, something outside of me happened. With an open mind during the acceptance prayer, I felt a fire run through my veins, and it was as if my arm lifted itself.

After H&I groups, I decided to journal for the day. I got interrupted again by Joel, but it was all good. We had an in-depth life talk, and I got the chance to fill him in on my past and how I ended here. He, too, ended up taking Jimmy on as a sponsor as well. The newest news is that the tech, Nick, got fired. I hadn't seen the guy in a minute. Not sure if it was because he was telling Joel things that were out of his authority or what. If I mess around long enough, I might end up with a job here.

Whelp… woke up at 5AM. It doesn't appear that I had been jerked off last night by Joel, but then again, I haven't had any action in a long while, so who knows? So, either the story is false, or Joel isn't into Iowa guys. Either way, I slept pretty well. What the Hell? Kris was up at 6:30AM eating a bowl of ice cream. This dude has yet to wake up before 8AM. Katrina came over and sat with us. I guess she got screwed over on leaving for a family funeral and is now leaving Friday.

Todd took off for clinicals around 8AM. Ol' Miss, Katrina, Wesley, and Duck Dynasty (Chaz) went with. I stayed back. Edwen finally brought his guitar, THANK YOU, and it was actually in decent shape. The bronze strings had seen some better days, and the bottom three were nylon. Some kind of Spanish or flamenco setup. I tuned it by ear and started to strum.

The action on the guitar seemed better than mine at home, and it sounded quite nice for not being touched in 10+ years. Then again, Cali ain't like Iowa, with the temperature change and nasty humidity. Edwen and Gwen seemed to dig my playing. It was nice to strum a bit, and to be sober on top of it.

I led first Group with Ty as my backup. We talked on giving of anonymous gifts. Why I actually started my nonprofit. Being that angel of hope in dark times. I'm there and gone, and hope it brings them faith in hard times. Probably ties into my love language of acts of service.

After first Group, I got to meet Miss Mary. She is from North Carolina, but she had moved to the U.S. from Kenya 18 years ago. A majestically beautiful woman, wow… Her eyes, smile, and sexy accent. Got this Iowa boy's heart going pitter-patter. She has a good nine years on me, but we connected quite well.

#1 RULE OF REHAB:
DON'T FALL IN LOVE IN REHAB!!!

But, seriously, though... Dang... This one is going to pull on my heart strings. I can tell this already.

While Edwen destroyed our cores at fitness class, George put together the new outdoor furniture that came in. Guess who claimed it before anyone else could sit on it? You got it... Ol' Hobble Bobble. Her and her 10,000 belongings. Can this woman go home already, for, like, the 20th time?

When we came out of Fitness, Ty took a second to introduce me to the new tech. Tony was his name, and he seemed like a pretty chill and respectable dude. He is fresh meat, though, so I guess we will see if he stays. Seems like turnover rate is quite high in this field. See if he sticks it out.

JoJo whipped up tacos for lunch. As usual, they were bomb. I finished off three tacos with about five scoops of ice cream before I took a breath. I couldn't imagine this being the reason I'm not losing any weight. Guess I will save that struggle for Phase 2.

After lunch, we piled in the old van and went to check out the new L.A. Rams stadium. Running out of things to do, and with the COVID shutdown, there aint a whole lot going on or open. See what this weekend brings. Hopefully, another trip to Booty Mountain, and I just might get lost there.

We couldn't get really close to the stadium, but the place is a modern-day work of art. I couldn't even imagine the scope of a project of this size. From there, we hit up Jamba Juice. Never had it before, but it was quite delicious and refreshing. It didn't hit me at first, but we were in Inglewood. Dr. Dre, where you at? We drove by where Nipsey Hussle was killed, and also the funeral home that hosted Tupac's funeral.

Some reason, Cheyanne wouldn't shut up. You could tell she was getting on George's last nerve. Some reason, she thinks she is bulletproof, and we thought she was going to get the van shot up. She was flipping people off and yelling out the window at people in the ghetto.

I told this dingbat chick she reminded me of a Chihuahua. A small and annoying creature you just want to kick to shut it up.

Not sure it resonated with her, but the rest of the van definitely was feeling me. Kris hollered from the back of the van, "Yo, George! Shut this b*tch up! I aint going out like this."

When we got back, Mary joined me by the fireplace cabana area. We have great conversations, and her smile is contagious. I had to cut it short and went to see Crystal in the office. My short-term disability was approved through August 11th for now. After finding this out, I went and talked to Cheryl about Phase 2. I figured instead of going home to a stimulus check and downtime, that I might as well stay with the treatment.

JoJo never ceases to amaze me. Buffalo, teriyaki, and BBQ chicken wings, with a fresh homemade slaw. Mary made the comment, "It will be hard to leave this cooking!"

You aint lying, girl. 50% of the reason why I probably stayed. Joel came out and was preaching the sober living home he was headed to. It's kind of hard taking advice from a lost, 25-year-old kid that just relapsed, and now is saying we don't need Phase 2. Seems he might be using the rehabs to see the world right now.

Shoot... I jotted it down backwards in my notes and in my journal. Before supper, I gave the topic of failure in our group to Edward. There was a lot of sharing, and the group in total got out some good feelings. We wrapped up the night with an uninteresting Zoom meeting. Everyone seemed pretty tired. Kris, Katrina and Cliff didn't even show for it.

I'm still having head pain, and my dumbass overdid my shoulders and back today, but... **NO TURNING BACK!**

What do they say, pain is gain and ultimately inevitable. I took my CBD for the night. Could use the more potent ones right now, for sure. Since the funeral of whomever, Nacho is in much higher spirits. Quite the laughing soul. Glad to have her back in better spirits, pretty sure she was overly stressed. I'm beat... Bedtime it is for this guy.

Woke up at 6:30AM. Of course, I forget it is U.A. day, and I took my morning piss. I think I remembered it once in 21 days... not too bad. New coffee group since Todd left. Now it's Cheyanne, Mary, and myself. It popped in my mind to draw a recovery triangle. I didn't think Cheyanne was going to shut her trap about the fact that she knew everything about healthcare, and her dad is this bigwig cop.

Sun was kicking by 8:15AM. From talk around the compound, I guess a heat wave is coming through. Still not all that bad, being it is dry heat. I lathered on some olive oil and grabbed my book. Some next level tanning. Nothing like a little vitamin D therapy and I am getting dark. Morgan came up while I was reading, with "good news." I was being transferred to Phase 2 today at 4PM. I guess my insurance wouldn't cover me at Phase 1 anymore. **NO TURNING BACK!** Let go and Let God.

During first Group with George, I got coined out. I thought I would be more emotional, but the group looked at me as a leader. I spit some truth on going from broken to driven. I also took ownership of leadership by example. I always helped, was there to listen, did chores, pushed myself in the workouts, read the AA book and kept my mind busy doing my journal at night.

Poor Mary was heartbroken I was leaving already. We were hitting it off pretty good. Our conversations were intimate, and we connected right off the bat. While getting meds, I played some guitar for MoMo and Evergreen. They really enjoyed it, and MoMo told me to find Adam when I got to Phase 2.

I killed it at open gym with Edwen. It was a bittersweet departure. Edwen seen I was driven, and he pushed me to excel. It was a good thing, too. JoJo doesn't stop bringing the heat. 21 days of some of the best cooking I have ever ate in my life. Today, it was a Mexi-style skirt steak with grilled zucchini, bell peppers, and eggplant. Not sure how he does it, or if quitting chewing has some effect, but I am eating everything, and it is fire.

1-3 PM, we had a meeting with Cheryl. Niko stopped in for the afternoon as well. It was good to hear she got her apartment figured out and doesn't have to get evicted. We did a worksheet on where we were headed. Everyone had similar writings. It was the mind of the addict. We ended the group by coining out Charise. Dang lady drove me crazy, but I had a spot in my heart for her. Although completely batshit crazy, she had me teary-eyed and she will be missed.

After the meeting, I packed up my stuff. Somehow, I acquired more than what my suitcase could hold. Afterwards, I had time to do the dishes one last time. Just my luck, Mary swung in. I got to show her the ropes in the kitchen. She wondered what she was going to do without me. Barely got a chance to break the ice and going to miss her dearly.

I swung over one last time to give Charley her last hug before my departure. I gave her a hug every hour from 9AM until 5PM when I left. She was scared with leaving tomorrow, and her anxiety was through the roof. I think she knows she is safe and taken care of at the compound, and in going home she knows that she isn't good or ready at all.

Moving on my favorite day… Cooking with JoJo. I tried just watching, but I soon jumped in and was hands on. I love the kitchen too much. I grabbed a few more numbers from people, hugs and some fist bumps, and it was off to Phase 2. The gal that picked me up seemed cool, and we had a good trip to the new house.

One of the first guys I met was good ol' Todd. The chick said I was going to have to strip and spread'em. I told her I was totally down, and she laughed it off. I don't think she expected me to be so willing. I figured there wasn't much I could do at that point.

Once checked in, I got the chance to tour the new compound. I got reunited with Todd, John, Angie, and Wesley was even there, too. One thing I spotted right off the bat was that someone had left a Mitchell guitar, and it was surprisingly in tune. Perfect, and thank you, Lord.

New place is actually compound-style and in the Encino territory. There is a brick wall all the way around the property, and out back there is an inground pool. I was thrown in a big-ass room with four beds, but I was told Monday I would be moving back to the guest house with John and Todd.

It was a cool little area with a kitchen area and three bedrooms, and it was close to the pool. Cool thing at Phase 2 is you can call every day, and they have a computer to do Zoom calls or Facetime on an iPad. Still no cellphones, but to tell ya the truth, I'm not actually missing the damn thing.

Surprisingly, I ended up getting a letter from my brother that they brought over from Phase 1. Our minds were alike. I thought he would have got my letter, but he hadn't yet. Hopefully, they arrive soon. It was good to see his kids in photos, and also to get their letters.

So far, the new house seems pretty chill. I ended the night catching back up with my peeps over some good ol' euchre. Always some good times throwing cards. See how this sleep goes and what tomorrow brings.

7-31-2020: (Friday): Meal Prep

B efore I went to bed last night, I called Amanda and the kids. Wanted to give them my new number that I would be calling from. I woke up at 5:15AM. Sleep wasn't all that bad, but it tended to be on and off. Some reason, my stomach was a little off; nothing out of the regular, though.

For some reason, the house only has two Brita water containers, and I think I could drink both. Surely was going to miss the water and ice machines from Phase 1. With it being quite a bit hotter in the valley, the house needs a water and ice machine. It's actually kind of ridiculous they don't have them, beings you can't drink the tap water.

I did my regular drawing at the kitchen table. After I was done, I decided to get a little workout in. I'm not sure when this Mike dude gets up, but he was already after it. The compound setup makes for a good, paved lap to jog. I came up with a three-set rotation with some free weights I found, and I was done by 7AM It was nice not waiting till 11AM, but it also sucks not having Edwen.

Side note: I got to meet Adam last night that MoMo told me about. He was a chill ex-military (Army) guy from Ohio. He was a country boy that lived outside the Cincinnati area, and he worked for FedEx. His story reminds me of my battles with my kids' mother. May just have some advice for the guy.

Sounds like when he leaves here, he is going into a war zone. Walking into a divorce going home. Wish the guy the best on an easy transition on returning home, and that he can focus on his sobriety. Who am I kidding, though? We got to go face the hell we created with a sober mind.

I guess a lot of people at the Phase 2 house are leaving. These businesses are quite the revolving door. After my workout, I read my book and practiced some guitar. I got to talk to Bradley. Cool gent from California. He struggles with opioids. He is in his early forties and digs water wells for a living. Sounds like he is on the divorce train, too.

The man seems extremely driven, and the switch is flipped to focus on his sobriety. He was to leave, but actually decided to stay longer. Hell, his truck is sitting in the driveway. If that doesn't take some willpower not to say, "Screw it!" and pack up when things get difficult, then I don't know what does. He is also down 50 pounds in almost 70 days.

We headed for clinicals with Darrell in the Mercedes van with the tech, Noah. Noah is a long-haired surfer boy, looking free spirit. It's like a give-and-take on nice things. At least this van had A/C. The drive was scenic and got to see some the Cali style homes. We pulled up on a 20-story building in a little downtown area.

Just my luck, the classes were on the top floor. Let's hope the A/C doesn't go out. I missed the first group to sign into the system for Phase 2. They ended up putting all our personal items in the secured office area in little lockers. I got to talking with Noah and found out he was from Missouri, and that he was actually quite a bit redneck.

I ended up making Darrell's part of Group, but something seemed off. Some reason, Wesley got on some higher thinking and ate up the time for the whole class. Patience, I guess... wasn't my day to relate or speak, but maybe someone got something from whatever the heck he was talking about.

We headed back to the compound for lunch. Talk about a s**t show. Twenty people all trying to make food at the same time. I cooked up eggs, spinach, and ham, with tater salad and chips. The kitchen is a rat race. I guess they didn't have a way to prep food at the offices, but in my mind, it would have made more sense to have food catered or something.

After lunch, Wesley and I were taken to West Hollywood for blood work of some kind with Adrian. Adrian was the house manager at Phase 2. Taller, heavy-set, emo type, but super friendly. The valley is scorching hot. It was 104 in Encino and only 86 at the West Hollywood location. Something about the mountains is what Adrian said.

West Hollywood compound was pretty cool, it just sat crammed in between two other buildings. I ended up reuniting with the Ohio chick, Sara, that gave me the colored pencils. Also ran into Travis. He was full of energy, but his face looked terrible... then again, my admissions pic was horrid.

I guess the blood work was for vitamin deficiencies and STDs. Figured I might as well know. Drunken nights... I have been a little rough on the little guy. Putting him places unprotected. Surprised the little guy didn't detach and leave me like everyone else. One thing I did notice was that West Hollywood had some cute chicks and an awesome pool. Probably why God didn't send me there.

Hell, I didn't realize it on the drive there, but we were on Sunset Strip in Beverly Hills. You could definitely sense the money in the area. Lots of exotic cars. Ferraris and Porsches were just common vehicles. One story that Adrian told on our way back to clinicals was very interesting.

He had a good friend and his girlfriend that went into the largest COVID test site in California. I guess their car started overheating, so they turned around about 40 minutes after they checked in. A week later, they received a letter in the mail saying they both tested positive for COVID, but the interesting thing was, they never got tested. Talk about a messed-up world pushing numbers to control the masses.

After clinicals, we came back home before the outdoor AA meeting in the park. I ended up taking a dip in the pool and got a second exercise in for the day. Got to get that beach bod after eating like a cow with JoJo. Angela marinated some chicken for tacos before we took off. This was definitely going to be different, cooking our meals, but I figured it would give a chance to show off my culinary skills.

The AA group was a neat experience. The first speaker was great. He did something that paralyzed him and messed up his brain. He ended up in AA. He now walks and talks normal. Dude was and is a miracle. The second speaker was his sponsee. Dude just rambled and it seemed the whole crowd lost interest. It didn't help he went over, like, 30 minutes.

On the way home, the old man, George, had the whole van going nuts. He kept playing with the radio, and he obviously had no clue what he was doing. When we got home, I threw the chicken on the grill. Angie made up a bomb-ass salsa from scratch. She also did a rice and black beans. We ate good and the house showed appreciation. It was at this moment Mama Bear (Angie) and I (Papa Bear) took over the kitchen for the whole house.

After supper, I helped with dishes, and I cut up pineapple and cantaloupe for the house to snack on. I was always looking for ways to stay busy, and I saw prepping food as just that opportunity. Plus, I saw a chance to reduce the rat race at lunch time.

I grabbed my CBD and hit the shower. My eyes were getting heavy, but I decided to keep up with my journal entry. I also rolled out my back for a bit outside on those foam workout rolls. It had been hurting pretty good all day. Not sure if there was a pressure front rolling through or I just tweaked it. Regardless, **NO TURNING BACK!**

8-1-2020: (Saturday): Malibu Canyon

Schedule has been kind of wack since coming to Phase 2, so I have been doing things out of order. Woke up at, like, 6:22AM and consumed a small breakfast. I made sure I called my parents around 8:45AM their time. Mother seemed to be happy to hear from me, and I got the chance to talk to Dad for a bit.

It was good getting to talk to both of them. Mom said that the letters finally arrived. Guess she was saying that they had Pops crying pretty good. He's getting softer in old age. They informed me they were starting to redo the deck with the polyboards. Not sure how the old man finds the energy and strength to still do all that crap.

I have been doing double workouts. The body said to take a break, so I let my mind convince me to do a workout. I didn't pull off a full three-set routine, but pretty close. The lower back is hurting again. Not sure why it acts up from time to time. The weather stays pretty consistent out here with pressure fronts not really changing.

Got the chance to connect/relate with Mike this morning. Odd character but seems like a good egg. He seemed to have a pretty rough upbringing, but at the moment seems spiritually centered. He is 37, no kids, and came from Florida. Found out he is into Buddhist theology, and he, too, had herniated discs in his back at a time. On top of, like, ten others in the house. We are just a bunch of broken people.

We headed for clinicals with Darrell at 9:15AM. We did a trust worksheet and then Kristal (tech who picked me up from Phase 1) ran a meditation on staying true to character. I shared I wanted to work on giving without expectation. Having expectation just sets one up for suffering.

We headed home at, like, 12:30PM with no plans till, like, 5PM. Angie said we needed to finalize the shopping list. Chad, the tech, would take 2-3 people on grocery shopping duties. I guess this was a Saturday night thing. Before COVID, everyone kind of bought their own food, but as of now, they shopped for the entire house. I think this was beneficial in Angie and I planning big meals. I smashed a fast lunch and joined Shakey Joe in the pool.

Joe is 25 and from New York. I guess he leaves Monday, and he is headed to Florida for a power line tech school or something. First question he had for me was what advice I had for him, and should he get married, when they all seem to fail these days.

His parents had divorced, and he got his heart broke along the way. Could definitely feel the walls he had in place. I told him not to worry too much about having life "figured out" at 25, but to just go pursue life. He said his dad put pressure on him because his twin brother's life is good. The house, job, dog, and girl.

We were called in the house, and we sang Kristal "Happy Birthday." They had cake and ice cream. John and I went back to the pool. I had definitely got enough sun for the day, but it was cool hearing Joe's story and getting to share mine with him before he left. I hope the best for the kid, and that he finds a new way of life while he is still young.

Hiking was optional, so only about half of us went. It was Noah, John, Todd, QP, Brian, Bradley, and me. QP is a young black man, I think, like, 23. He is the goofball of the house. He is always sleeping in Groups. He ran with gangs and got tied into drugs. I guess now he is trying to be the next big rapper. Supposedly, he was training MMA but punched a window and broke his wrist. Seems like he is saving face instead of ass, but who knows.

Malibu Canyon didn't fail in its beauty. It just looked like some deserty hills at first, and then it opened up into gorgeous cliffs. It looked like where *Jurassic Park* was filmed. That or like *Lord of the Rings*. We headed down a dirt trail through a valley.

We crossed a dried-up river and made our way to a little isolated pond. It was a secluded little scene. One that you would see Bob Ross paint in one of his fun little episodes on public television. Absolutely stunning, surrounded by beautiful mountains.

We ran into four chicks in bikinis and that helped increase the scene.

Noah was all about taking pictures with some awesome backdrops. We saw lizards, squirrels, and rabbits. No snakes, which didn't hurt my feelings in the least. On the way back, I got to talk to Big Brian from Alabama. He is 47, sells cars as a profession, and lives in the backwoods. He was in the Marines and got medical discharge. Guy fell out of a helicopter that had got shot down, from about forty feet up in the jungles of Columbia.

I guess his group was directly tied into the D.E.A. and they came in shortly after Pablo Escobar was killed. He said when he hit the ground, he had been shot through the shin. I guess they packed it full of cocaine, and when that s**t hits the blood, you feel absolutely nothing. Beings they were in the middle of the jungle with no first aid, the cocaine also worked as a disinfectant for the wound.

After service, he got into coke and chasing women. He worked in car sales for like twenty years and was now semi-retired. I guess now he sells cell phones for Sprint because he got bored selling cars. I know he said he buried his son in Groups. This guy has definitely been through hell and back.

We finished our hike with him and I walking up the dried-up river bed. We were looking for cool rocks. I guess it was a hobby of Brian's to collect cool stones. Noah got on us about heading back. I guess anything after 8PM in the park and it was a $71 fine.

When we returned home, I had had enough being outside for the day. I was burnt to a crisp. I called my son quickly and it seemed like things were chill with him. It has been some time, but for me it has gone super-fast. I can't wait to get to see both of them again. I talked with Amanda quick, too. Parents had paid my rent, and Dad had thrown in an extra $400 because he says, "Don't worry about it."

It's a peace of mind, knowing my bills are caught up. I am 110% grateful for my family keeping things locked down at home. Amanda said my son is looking to move in with me and possibly go to school in my area. The big man definitely knows what he is doing. I needed sobriety for the next phase and blessings to occur in my life. **NO TURNING BACK!**

I threw together a quick supper, and I took the initiative to do some housecleaning. Obviously, the chore board meant nothing, and staff wasn't holding people accountable. I mopped the kitchen, dining room, and living room. My back was screaming. Sunday will definitely be a stretch out day.

The squad came back with groceries, and they weren't joking. They dropped over $1000, and it was pretty evident. Everything is packed to where you can barely shut cupboards and fridge/freezer doors. And to think, they do this every Saturday or something. Angie, Adam, and Mike went ham.

I met up with Adam, Brian R, Chad, and Noah in the garage. I played some guitar, and Adam did a reading from a book. I told them the story of accepting Jesus and feeling the fire at the Tipton church. They all got goosebumps. I had to call it a night, for the CBD kicked in. Add that to all the sun I got, and I was whooped. I hit the showers and zonked out. Some reason, these weird people always fall asleep to watching horror movies. I switch it up to Indian flute music, just to mess with them.

8-2-2020: (Sunday): Zuma Beach and a Grill Out

I woke up the latest I have since I have been in California. My back has been on absolute fire. Definitely missing my high-power CBD gummies, but pool relaxation and easy workouts should help. My schedule was a little off. I didn't draw or exercise as I usually do. Mike woke up early and prepared a breakfast for everyone. I took initiative to do dishes before heading to clinicals.

First Group was with a guy named John who was originally from Council Bluffs, Iowa. He shared a cool video about choosing God's will. That he doesn't take the driver's seat but gives us road maps to follow. After that, we all got to pick a song that John played. We also had to explain why we chose it, once the song was over.

Cool meeting, and also cool meeting another Iowa native. My song was Casting Crowns's "East to West." I chose this song because it is one of my favorite Christian groups. I also chose it for the lyric, "I don't want to see the man I've been, come rising up in me again." Very powerful lyric relating to my current life.

The next group, we did a C.R.A.S.H. report with Noah and Adrian. I swear all this QP kid does in groups is sleep and definitely not participate. It would be nice if the staff actually did something, but… ultimately, it is his recovery, and they are still getting paid. We then piled back in the vans for the lunch scramble. We had till like 5PM. Sometimes, later classes got cancelled, due to COVID crap. People still thought they all needed to eat at the same time. I guess the place was completely stock on food.

I decided, since I had the time, that I grilled the pork sirloins. I did half-BBQ and
half-spicy, and I also whipped up a fresh Pico de Gallo. About an hour in, I wrapped them in foil to retain the moisture. They shredded right off the bone, so I laid out BBQ pulled pork and pork carnitas. Safe to say, the house devoured it.

About 4:30PM, I called my daughter and asked her how the

skate party went. Seems like she had a good time. Seems both kids spent, like, five days with Lauren and Levi. Not sure what their mom is doing, but I got a good idea she is chasing a new guy, and not in the picture of taking care of them. I'm glad my kids are older now and just pray they stay safe.

We then took off (well, five of us) for Zuma Beach. The drive was absolutely stunning once you got past the fear of an early death, because Kristal can't drive. It was like a scene from *Need for Speed*. We wound through mountains with no shoulders on the road, just straight off the mountainside. We also went through tunnels that were lit up. I was definitely in awe.

The beach ended up being decently populated for 5:30PM. It was a bit hazy, but still a nice vibe. Crazy we went from 100 at the house to 70 degrees at the beach in just 20 miles. Kristal decided to hit the water, and QP joined her. I finally decided to say, "F**k it!" and joined as well. The water is freezing. It is like instant hypothermia. Kristal said this is where ya let go of all the bad energies as an empath.

Well, what a great day to be an empath. I guess once I got in the water, it wasn't all that bad. High tide came in and the waves were kicking. Nothing like the gulf. We had 6-10ft waves crashing in. At about 50 feet out, I was diving through waves 4-6 feet over my head. I ended up seeing a sea lion, a dolphin, some fish, and I found a cool, flat black rock to give Big Brian.

The drive home was a little more nerve-racking, for damn sure. Kristal didn't understand how to use defrost and/or the windshield wipers. With the high tide coming in, it made for dense fog going back through the mountains. Old boy George in the front seat let Kristal have it and hit the wipers. I think we all had crap in our pants and Kristal was acting like nothing was wrong. Luckily, a third of the way up, the mountain the fog just disappeared. George was still chewing out Kristal. He had us all cracking up. Kristal wouldn't pull the van over, so Mike took it upon himself to piss in a bottle. I'm not sure how Steve didn't have a heart attack. He is a big dude, probably 6'3", 350 lbs. He drank two Bangs and a coffee in, like, two hours. Glad I quit the shit with alcohol and nicotine.

Some reason, after me cooking, they still ordered three pizzas and chicken wings. Somehow, they all got smashed. I didn't eat any. Got a new guy from West Hollywood. Michael, from Tennessee, seems like a pretty cool guy. He seems to be into working out. I ate supper with George. He, too, has an awesome backstory. He had a rough upbringing in the Chicago territory. Gangs, drugs, and guns. Said he got tired of being scared. He joined the Army. His dad was a WWII vet, and he went to Vietnam.

I packed away food, did dishes, and then Adam helped buzz my head. Adam is a great guy. I got to talk to him while I grilled. He is about to go through divorce and a custody battle. I wish the best for him and glad he is staying longer to better himself in knowing he isn't prepared to go home. His ex sounds just like my kids' mom.

She knows what she did and does. I'll leave it there... just in case she is to read this one day. No need to throw shade. I will make sure I trade numbers with Adam. Adam will face some eye-opening shit he can't control, and if needed, hopefully I can be of some service.

I let go of thinking I need to draw, read, and write every day. Just need to double up the next, or not. Life has been getting busy, and that pool and grill be calling my name. I popped some CBD and ibuprofen for the back. I did a short workout and called it a night. Note to self: always pray before riding with Kristal.

8-3-2020: (Monday): Revolving Door

Woke up a little stiff, and not talking about in my boxer shorts. The Buddhist state that pain is temporary. I'm not sure if they are relating it to life is temporary, but Lord, I could use some relief. I promise I am being good. Bradley and Mike were already exercising.

Thank God they were, because it pushed me to change clothes and get some sets in. I have been jogging but my wind is still weak. Could use me one of those ellipticals I said I would never be caught dead on. After my back injury, the low impact is more than appealing to this man.

Mika, the tech drove us to clinicals, and this guy is cool company. Got to be grateful for this staff I have been blessed with. In **NO TURNING BACK**, the Lord is guiding my journey. Some days I wonder, but I am soon reminded.

Mika played his own tracks in the van. The dude is actually quite the rapper. The first he played sounded liked it came straight off the radio, but he was down talking it as garbage. Self-talk can be dangerous, and I hope he gains the confidence. I could see this kid blowing up on the music scene.

Mika is a recovered addict, and he led our first meeting on trust. A lot of us came to realize we couldn't trust our own selves in addiction. We realized we once gave too much trust, and now our walls have us not trusting anyone.

Second Group was with Tracey. At first take, I like this guy. He is funny but runs a tight ship, and he is very professional in his actions. He definitely aint afraid to tell someone to shut up. I guess he is one of the head program directors or something. Kind of hard saying who is who at this place.

In Tracey's group, we had to bring up things we avoid. My first things were easy. My health, wealth, goals and so on. My next tugged at the heart strings, but I'm glad I shared them. I shared I had a third child that I had never met. As time goes on, it seems to keep getting harder. Tracey seemed to understand my issue and its complexity, but also said my made-up future was all in my head. That in meeting him it would be emotional, but also quite simple.

After Group, we hit the lunch scramble. Part of me just wants to start skipping it. Seems like I was always one bite in, and then being pushed out the door. We piled back in the vans, and back to clinicals we went. Third Group was Breath Work with Sam, and just my luck, right after lunch once again. I still haven't got back to when I did it the first time, and I couldn't tell you why.

Fourth Group was PsychoEd with Don. I asked what he was about, and most of the group said he does nothing. Today, God humbled those folks. He brought a defense mechanism study, and noticing our shadows. Everyone seemed to dive into the discussion, and we fed off one another's energy. Adam and Sara were psyched because he played "Forty Six & 2" by Tool. It just so happens that Tool is Adam's favorite band.

We headed home and I knew I was pool bound. About the time I went to plop down in the pool, the pool cleaning guy showed up. Which it was much needed, due to algae overgrowth. After cleaning, he stated no swimming for 24 hours due to shocking the water. It was all good, though. It gave me time to relax for a bit in bed.

5:30PM, we headed to the AA group in the park. One lady had over 40 years sobriety. The people who shared all did awesome. Hell, Bradley took the time to share. He broke down and started crying, but he pulled it back in. Proud of the guy. He even decided to stay longer because he knew he wasn't ready to go home. All in all, I am surrounded by some great people.

We came home, and Angie and I threw down a feast. We did oven-baked salmon, a fresh salad, and quinoa. I grilled up burgers. The house smashed it... except Mike... he had to cook for himself. He saw it was done, he didn't grab any, and then he threw a guilt trip about us not saving any for him.

The guy, at times, gets very self-serving and jealous. He will complain about people claiming food, yet the guy had like six bags of his own groceries that no one was allowed to touch. He got to go shopping and was on food stamps. If that aint some entitled shit. Hey, Bro! You are buying food with tax dollars. Get over us eating your stash.

Learning, sometimes, you just got to go with the flow. Pick-your-battles kind of game show. We got another dude from West Hollywood. He seems pretty chill. I will see what he is about tomorrow. I got some time to myself... odd... I called Jimmy earlier. I'm trying to get him to the house, but they keep flagging him on some COVID protocol. I'll probably finish off the night reading my book. Note to self: When George farts, it hangs around for a couple days.

8-4-2020: (Tuesday: New Dad

Woke up to an overcast sky, and it was pretty cool to top that. It made for a nice workout. The back was finally feeling decent, so I got some good sets in. When we got to clinicals, I took a minute to talk with Tracey. For what it was worth, he said they would fit me in, address some situations, and get in touch with my sponsor.

I'm not real sure why I always seem to get pushed to the side, but it is what it is, and I have a newfound faith in things working out. I need to be less selfish when focus is on others. I know God is with me, but at times I get frustrated and focus on problems instead of the solutions.

First Group was with Noah, and we discussed our secrets. Other than my third child, which I had come to realize was broken promises and denial, I had hidden from my problems. I promised my children things and never came through. Things like this definitely pulled on my heart strings and gave me a sense of worthlessness.

Second Group was with Saeed. Saeed was an old Mexican dude that appeared high on life, cocaine, or two pots of coffee in. Came to find out he was a recovered coke addict. He did an energetic talk on finding purpose. It reminded me a lot about "The Secret" on Netflix about the law of attraction, that my daughter had me watch.

We headed back home for the lunch scramble. I'm learning to hold off, like, ten minutes, and then make something small just to tide me over. I don't have a bag to do the snack game like Mike and Angie. We headed back for Fighting Chance with Chad. He was a proud new father to a healthy baby girl. Today he went more in depth on combos. Just so happens we did it on the roof of the building and it was miserably hot. We did a double left jab, right hook, duck back, right uppercut, left hook, and ended with a cross body right.

We got a little break once we got home, so I hit the pool for some suntan/meditation time. After bronzing the dad bod, I teamed up with Angie to prep dinner. I cut veggies for salad, did some poor man's garlic bread from hot dog buns, and grilled chicken. While the coals were still hot, I threw down some hot dogs for lunch rush. Angie did shrimp Alfredo pasta.

Mike threw a fit yesterday about not getting food when he walked away, and then the guy did the same thing today. He watches as we finish dinner yet, is so "me-oriented" that he gets in our way to make up some herbal tea concoction, and then walks away leaving the stove on.

He then whips up a pre-workout drink and decided to go full on exercise, five minutes before supper is served. The whole time you can tell he did it on purpose with the intentions of letting us hear about it later that night or the next morning. In fixing food for "everyone," I had to let go of the anger building in me.

Last group of the night was with Gabe. First experience with the dude, and he is hilarious. Guy should do stand-up comedy. His words just flow so naturally. He speaks realness and gives insight on the realities of addiction, and where your mind will lead you when left to your own devices.

Ol' George kept the laughs going. Some dance, cash missing off a table, in a room with a gal, putting his safety in her hands, and then skating because the gang wanted to whoop him. (You gotta experience a George story to get the real effect.)

I took time to finish up the book, *Against the Stream.* The end was pretty cool. How Buddha didn't want people to follow "A" religion, but to create their own life and spiritual journey. That we tend to just get stuck in copying others and miss out on our purpose and our own growth. "Be the change you wish to see in the world." Odd this is a photo I have shared on my nonprofit page.

We then gathered for euchre. Of course, I get stuck with Angela going against Todd and John. Angie surprises me all the time as my partner. One hand, it seems she doesn't have a clue, and the very next hand, she goes alone and completely plays it wrong, but still lucks out and wins. When one has both bowers and a queen, one tends not to play the queen right then, not knowing where the ace and king are at. We gave our best shot but lost by two.

I finished off the night by passing off the book I just finished to Mike and then did a drawing. I need a lot more refining but doing a tattoo concept for the recovery triangle. Part of me wants to incorporate my sobriety date... I will sleep on it for a while. Totally due for some ink therapy. I will have to see how financials go, once I get back home.

8-5-2020: (Wednesday): LA Zoo Hike

Woke up to another overcast morning. I ate a small breakfast. This fatty needs to start cutting back calories. Somehow, I ended up at 210lbs. I was like 201lbs at Phase 1. Still trying to figure out where I packed on ten pounds. I'm shorter, just a little wider than some of the guys here. For some reason they are all 185's, and my chunky ass has 25 pounds on them.

I called Amanda while no one was awake. I figured out my financial situation, and totally forgot about getting a bonus check. I'm still not sure on when my short-term disability is going to start getting deposited. The kids' mom is asking about child support already... Must be in need of highlights in her hair and her nails done. It is what it is, and a resentment I'm having to learn to accept and let go.

We headed to clinicals in the Mercedes van. I had Michael (tech) play some "They Might Be Giants." Mike actually knew the band and started singing along. Just when you think you are the only one... First Group was with Kristal. I got pulled out by Tracey after the first topic.

First topic was a good one. It was on love. I brought up the book about love languages. It's a great read on how people give and receive love. Some in the group had read it and some hadn't. I actually read it after divorce. I've always had great timing in relationships.

Second group was with Big Book Mike. He is a really cool guy that has battled 25 years with addiction. He has had some cool jobs, too. He actually worked for Star Magazine. Said he got sent all over Hollywood/LA to interview and take pictures of the stars at parties. I guess he lived in New York for like eight years, and you could definitely hear it in his voice. At the end of group, he thanked me for bringing the fire to the discussion.

Not sooooo much of a lunch scramble today because our next thing was a hike at 1:30pm. Gave us a good two hours to settle in.

I ate small then went out to tan/nap-itate, (the act of meditation napping.) We then headed for Griffith Park. I didn't realize the back side of it was the old LA Zoo.

We hiked with Mika. He chose the spot, and it was a great workout. I guess Mika is taking Reno (stage 2 facilitator) skydiving Saturday. This is something I want to try sometime. From there we drove up close to the Hollywood sign, and we all took pictures. There were a couple of girls there that reminded me of my daughter. They were doing TikTok dances in front of the big Hollywood sign. Won't lie... kind of wanted to hop in and show off my moves.

We came home, and even after the exhausting hike, I got a workout in. I went hard, too. Cars were blocking the driveway, so I incorporated sprints down the length of the compound. Mike dropped one of the dumbbell's weights and it broke so I had to adapt to a one-dumbbell workout. I'm starting to feel better and show definition. It just sucks because I am ten pounds heavier than when I showed up.

We headed for AA meeting at the park. Found out something interesting... so the new young black kid, Tre, was at West Hollywood ATC with Tray, the white dude, from Phase 1. I guess the tranny chick, Gwen, that jumped ship from stage 2 house was back at West Hollywood. Just so happens, Tray decided to hit on her/him. They didn't tell him; they just let him go for it. They said they tried warning him and he just brushed them off. I guess that's what the kid gets for making stuff up about Joel, but then again, maybe the dude is just young and naïve... who knows?

When we got home, Angie threw down a beef stroganoff. It was damn tasty, too. Adam also helped with dinner as well. I told myself no cooking and just relax. As soon as supper was over, I was meal prepping for breakfast. Ham, egg, and cheese in a muffin tin. I taste tested one... Fire! Trying to beat the everyday hustles. Hopefully, I made enough for the house.

Woke up to another cloudy day. The body was feeling decent. Back is still aching, but it seems to be a more centralized pain. I started off the day by putting away dishes, and I mopped the kitchen, living and dining room areas, while people slept. I woke up at 5:10AM, for some reason. People have been getting really lazy. Some people are taking pre-workouts, just to sit on the couch all day. I'm not sure if they got moms that still wipe their butts or what.

I reheated my egg muffins I prepped last night, and they got smashed fast. The one dude told me I should start a restaurant. While eating a small breakfast, I read the *Daily Reflections* and *24 Hours a Day* readings. We then packed in the Ford Transit, nuts to butts, and headed to clinicals with Michael.

First Group was morning meditation with Mika. I had a 9:30AM meeting, so I missed it. I saw Stefany, and we talked on my third child and a conference call with my parents. Trying to lay down some knowledge on expectations. She did say she would reach out to Reno about getting me into the doctor or ENT about my head issue. Would be nice to not have vertigo feeling all the time. I want to trust this woman, but for some reason, my gut still doesn't agree with Stefany.

I came back in to Second Group with Big Book Mike, and we were doing improv comedy scenes. It was a cool concept, and it made for many good laughs. We headed home for the lunch scramble, and Mika got time extended to 12:45PM, so we weren't rushing. I ate quickly and jumped into bed for a quick nap. I must have time warped. I woke up real groggy.

We came back to clinicals to group with Stefany. She did a video I had seen by Renee Brown on vulnerability, and we did worksheets on what we were vulnerable about. Growing up, I wasn't taught or shown it, that's for damn sure. A lot of it came from having kids… especially my daughter.

During break, I talked with Adam, and we both had frustrations about the staff doing their jobs. Some people were in the offices of Reno, Tracey, or another counselor every day. Both him and I had to advocate for ourselves to be seen. Maybe it is just another test from God.

Groups went well, and everyone wholeheartedly expressed themselves. God is good! In **NO TURNING BACK**, the good Lord aligned me with a great group/family of people that all feed off one another. Upon arriving back home, Adam and I hit a workout. My typical schedule has been thrown off. I haven't been drawing, but I cook a lot now. I draw when inspired to, but love being of service to others in the house. I hopped in the pool for a quick bit before Gabe and I put together some new outdoor furniture.

Our last Group was awesome. Big Mike brought in Chuck from Arkansas with 112 days sober, and Henry from Miami that knew Mike for over seven years. Chuck was one of those handyman people. We found a leak in the kitchen sink, and he had it fixed before meeting started. This was Chuck's first time giving his testimony, and God definitely had him in the right place at the right time.

Both Chuck and Henry had been thru hell, and they both found the light to a better life. Henry was an awesome speaker, and I got his info, in that going to Florida I would reach out to him. The AA family seems pretty awesome. Maybe Mom was right in saying that I would travel the U.S., telling my story. Hell, maybe my son might be right, too, in that my journal/book would become a New York Times bestseller. Only time will tell.

Toward the end of our meeting, the sober living dudes swung through. It's always nice seeing familiar faces. I threw burgers and chicken wings on the grill. It tends to be my go-to spot at night. For not cooking on charcoal, I got that son of a bitch figured out pretty quick. Been getting good smoke and not drying the food out.

We ended the night listening to Tre spit bars. I will give it to the kid... He has talent, and to think he has only been spitting for, like, two years. Bradley (Brett Favre) rolled in late. I thought he was with his sponsor. I guess Chaz came in on his day off, and took him to see his son. This was awesome, and you could see the glow on his face.

Woke up to the news on and everyone tuned in. There were helicopters flying over our compound. No shit, a guy in a high-speed chase was shot dead just blocks from our house. I guess he had, like, five fully automatic weapons on him. Kind of scary, but not so much. Kind of get used to it. There are always cop helicopters flying overhead, and we are in LA... F**king Hollywood.

Took the time to write yesterday's entry. I have been slacking on journaling and drawing. I found my spot in the house, and by the time it's writing time, it's 10:30PM and I am spent. Making sure, though, to jot some notes down throughout the day.

Had our first group with Noah at clinicals. I don't really remember what it was about. Everyone seemed tired and worn out from all the relations and conversations being made and had. Just seemed like everybody was physically and emotionally drained.

Second Group was with Darrell, and I ended up letting go. I had some skeletons to get off my chest. I understand that everyone's recovery is their own process, but when a person becomes a distraction and a disservice to the entire group... the staff doing absolutely jack squat... I felt I had no other option than to be assertive. Darrell actually completely agreed with me, and a lot of people thanked me for having the courage to speak out. Darrell liked when I said, "Give me some psychology books and I'll read them, and tell y'all how to do your jobs better!"

I'm accountable for my recovery. The staff should be accountable, and will be held accountable to do their end as long as I am up in these rooms... That's for damn certain. I have learned every job I ever had and did it with excellence. They are fools to think I'm afraid to call B.S. on staff not holding up their end of the bargain.

I gave my will up! I turned the keys of my life over to your staff, the professionals... Do your jobs! Group ended up getting lively and everyone started to participate. Darrell did kick QP out before Group started, for sleeping. I gave him dibs, and he expressed creating positive boundaries.

We did the lunch scramble, and when we returned back to clinicals, Wesley was back. I guess he said he had to sign divorce papers or something. We then had an accountability group with Tracey. (Side note – I know staff gets overly busy, but they can't forget current clients over new ones.) He did a question box. Mine was something I had trouble letting go of. I brought up Skylar.

My dog was my girl. She was my love and friend when I had none. Moving into an apartment, being all alone, and to top, no dog to comfort my anxieties… It absolutely killed me. Everyone agreed and Tracey really felt what I was spitting. I still had a resentment of Amanda (ex-wife) giving up Skylar to her brother, and then turning around and replacing the dog immediately with another dog. Then she had the audacity to tell me, "I couldn't live without this dog. Now I know why you loved Skylar so much."

We headed back home, and I tried to go for a swim. Bradley and I were met by Adrian, and he asked if we could assemble the new grill. We destroyed that b*tch! Adrian said he would buy us Fat Sal's for building it. The grill was nice and, big plus, it was gas. It will be great for the grill out tomorrow evening.

At 5:30PM, we left for the AA meeting at the park. I got my 30-day chip. It's the first time I have been sober for 30 days since I was 14. We came home and I cooked breakfast for the house. Big Brian whipped up some badass scrambled eggs.

I ended the night with an upper body workout. No days off and **NO TURNING BACK!** I headed out to the garage and did some strumming with Gabe. He actually knew some guitar. The CBD kicked in and I was ready to call it a night after the late workout.

I came in and talked crazy baby mamas with Adam. He is about to head into a hell I have been beaten down ruthlessly by. I had him in awe with some of the stories that I told him about what the kids' mom and her family had pulled. All I could say was I'm still here kicking, and trying to be a better person. Told him he had my number and that he could call me whenever. I knew that battle all too well and the toll it takes on a person.

8-8-2020: Saturday: Mary's B-day Party

I woke up super late (7:40AM), and it felt super good. It's nice on weekends that clinicals don't start until later. We leave around 9:15AM. After breakfast I called Mom and Dad to check in. Mom was busy cleaning, and Dad was tearing off boards on their main deck to replace it with composite boards. Not sure how the ol' man still does it. Body is broken, smoke and drank like 50 years, and the ol' cat just keeps on going.

Groups were with Darrell and Kristal, and they were on the spiritual side. Mike, a black male in his thirties, went in on his life of gangbanging to QP and Tre. Mike got emotional and teared up. The whole room could feel his pain and resentment. The luxury life it shows in music videos comes with a high price and mind manipulation. He realized he had the power of choice.

Brian (old Marine) ended by throwing down some old wisdom. He praised their talents, but he reiterated that if they tried to go back where they came from, death was inevitable. It definitely was the best group to date. I think in stepping out and showing I was serious about recovery, and that I wouldn't put up with disrespectful antics, that other people started to be more vulnerable and speak out.

Patience is key! The Lord hears your prayers! I am witnessing the power and miracles of his works. The vibe is changing for the better in the rooms, and it is something I had prayed on. Like Bradley is saying... We are all children of God. We must pray for our brothers and sisters for a better way of life. We can't get caught in anger and be quick to judge books by their covers. Like the book I read (*Against the Stream*), we must separate the actor from the actions.

Darrell's talk was on trust, and my analogy on it related to a bank. Fear tends to be stronger than love in people. They say to trust no one. Even your own blood will screw you over. I looked at it as a credit line. People come to your "Bank of Trust." Until proven untrustworthy, the people credit score goes up. So as a human, we trust another with a higher credit line. We give this trust to new people, and their actions reflect their credit score. Credit/trust can be lost, but also rebuilt.

We were done for the day. I skipped lunch and hit a workout. I knew supper was going to be filling. Wesley got stuck in his own mind. He isolated and then he took off again, just up and out of the blue. I hope the best for the guy. I jumped in the pool thereafter. The sun was beaming down. Nice little cool down while doing my laundry.

Angie and I started prepping food for the party. Give this man a knife and food to cut up, and I am in my happy place. I got Adrian to agree on a rib night this coming Thursday, and got to where Mike could make his mac 'n' cheese. I guess they used to do big meals once a week that the business paid for. Adam said he was down to do his own take on ribs.

The new grill was awesome. The bone-in with skin-on chicken flared up a bit, but past that, it grilled like a champ. Big Joe from Phase 1 helped me grill. The party went awesome. It was great seeing old faces, especially Mary's. I missed the girl. We did a birthday cake and sang her Happy Birthday. Big Joe showcased his guitar and singing talent. Guy was pretty impressive. Guess he was in a family band back in Washington.

Even though it was Mary's birthday, she insisted on giving me a massage for orchestrating all the cooking. I finally gave in! Her hands felt magical on my tight muscles. We said our goodbyes to people, and Phase 1 piled up in the van and took off. I gave Mary double hugs. From the way it sounds, she won't be doing Phase 2 and just be headed home. We exchanged numbers and she asked that I stay in touch.

Edward remembered the book. It was more than I expected. It was a self-discovery/worksheet book. It came right when I had no more to read. Before they took off, I grabbed Ty and Edwards's cell numbers so I could keep in touch. God is good! He never leaves your side. Special thanks to Phase 1 for buying way too much food. We got cooked meat for all next week. I guess we have Phase 1 people coming over soon.

I called Madison (daughter) to see if she got the hiking pictures I sent, that Noah took at Malibu Canyons. I found out she had an iPhone 8, so I Face-timed her from the iPad. It was great to see her face. She got highlights in her hair and she looked beautiful… Just growing up way too fast. Like Kenny Chesney's song, "Don't Blink." It aint no s**t. Life will pass one by if you don't stay in tune. **NO TURNING BACK!**

I grabbed up the guitar and learned a few new songs off the computer in the garage. I came to find out they busted Cheyenne from Phase 1 for stealing from our Phase 2 house during the cook-out. She ganked all kinds of stuff. I will pray for her, but it doesn't look good for her recovery in creating a huge distrust among the people. It was odd… Right before they left, I said don't go crazy and go home on me. She seemed skittish, and gave me a quick hug… Makes sense now.

I ended the night in the garage with Adam and Chaz talking about the benefits of CBD, Cheyenne, and the system breaking these kids over the past, like, thirty years. It's sickening, all the narcotics and body brokering that is pushed on human life to put money in the hands of criminals. On that note, time for a hot shower, prayer, and bed.

Going back and forth on this sleep schedule. Woke up early this morning. Around 5AM or so. I cooked up some left-over taters, brats, and eggs with some hot sauce. Mike's crazy self was up sewing something at the dining room table. I'm not sure how much shit this guy has, but I think he has more things in his closet than I have in my apartment.

I started doing my journal and it hit me… Mop the floors while no one is stirring around the compound. I mopped the main house floors and the back house main floor. Nice that Chuck (Arkansas dude from sober living) fixed the leak on the sink and adjusted the hose to fill the mop bucket easier. I then sat down and finished my journal entry and read the daily reflection and 24-hour books. I shared the one with Adam about giving up power and control.

I went outside and started with some yoga style stretching. Beings it was Sunday, I was just going to stretch out, but… it turned into a full body workout. I joked with John when we got in the van that I got more done before he woke up than he would do all day. Well… actually, not joking. Got to be hungry for recovery.

First Group was with Council Bluffs. We watched part 4 about making a moral inventory with some older priest dude that owns a rehab facility. We then went into music therapy. I had the song, "Cold," by Crossfade, but it switched to Casting Crowns's "Praise You in This Storm." By the time it got to me, I chose, "No Roots." In Facetiming my daughter, I'm realizing I miss my princess. She's the main girl in my life that keeps me grounded. That song is our jam.

It also relates in that, leaving home at 18, I never had my "own" place. My last relationship, every argument came down to… It was her house and if I didn't like it my kids and I had to pack up and leave. Even though married and all the blood, sweat, and tears I put into the place to make it a home, that I was just some pawn in the house being pushed around. Something I will make damn sure never happens again.

Noah came for last meeting. Half the group did a guided 40-minute meditation, and the other half did worksheets of some kind. I just napped and it felt great. I guess I was snoring, but I know Mike I. was super-breathing. I just can't do it. Lay there and listen to some boring, methodical speaker with a full belly. I don't get out of my mind. My mind just shuts down, but I stay coherent in a sense. Guess that is probably what the body and mind needed. Sorry to everyone if they were actually trying to full body meditate.

<u>8-10-20: Monday: Monday Morning Blues</u>

Monday morning blues were in go mode. I had a sense of being home. After speaking with the daughter, I got a little homesick, to say the least. My kids are lost right now, and their protector and leader is gone bettering himself, and their mom seems to be more interested in finding her next sugar daddy.

Hotel-hopping with guys she just met, and going on drinking binges while leaving the older kids to fend for themselves. My daughter told me she cried for two days straight because she missed me. My son is mad at the world, and fed up with his mom. Guess the apple doesn't fall too far from the tree. I guess he has only been "home" ten minutes in, like, two weeks. Just staying with friends and as far away from the mess as possible.

What can appear to some as a vacation from reality can actually be hell on Earth. In times like these, I want to be there, but I also know I need to be good with my sobriety before entering this war zone. Let go and let God, for sure! I will pray for love in the kids'/family's hearts, and that they stay safe. Also, for God's will, in knowing he has greater plans for my children and myself. **NO TURNING BACK!!** This definitely fuels the fire for the redemption of my life.

Morning meditation was with Mika. Found out on the way to clinicals that Chaz, Adrian, Mika, and Reno all play C.O.D. Warzone. I will be trading some gamer tags, for sure. Figure I should only have about fifty hours of updates when I get home. That is, unless it automatically updated. If ya know, ya know! QP was up and going for meditation... that was new to Group. I guess Mika and Reno are going skydiving this weekend.

Second Group was with Tracey. I popped in quick and spoke to Reno. I found out no vitamin deficiencies and no STDs. Crossing my fingers, fox hole prayers, or a high concentration of alcohol in the system must have kept me clean. Then again, one doesn't typically engage in a lot of promiscuous sex while strapped to an XBOX. So, a big thank you to social distancing and online gaming.

I'm drawing blank on what we talked about with Tracey. Had to be something that didn't interest QP because he was instantly sleeping. Mike did a timeline. Hell of a backstory. This guy has about done it all. He had the whole room in tears when he got to the part when his father passed away. Man has witnessed a lot of death and troubles in his life.

We took a short break, and we came back and coined out Mike. My gift in the coin was best wishes and anger management. I totally get the quickly being angered, but the kicking stuff and throwing fits at 38 years old is a little much. Starting a family and having some kids will help with his patience, but with his schooling, it may be a few years yet.

Back to the regular lunch scramble and back to Breath Work with Sam. I hyped myself up and said a prayer to give me an open mind... and Gosh Darn it... It Worked! I didn't fall asleep, tears entered my eyes, and at the end it felt as if something crawled out of my body and left my presence. Which my topic in mind was letting go of past resentments and breaking down the walls. Like they say in AA, "It works if you work it!"

We then had a meeting with Reno, Adrian, Mika, and Noah. *House Rules!* They agitated a lot of people, but coming from a big company, I totally understood management's side on things. It's hard to pick and choose, so it has to be pretty cut and dry, black and white. There can be no in between.

House chores, garage off limits, blah blah blah. The management wasn't really holding up their side. They had a white board with names and chores on it. I think myself and two of the girls are the only ones that clean. I chose to speak up on chores extending to vehicles. A house full of men, and we don't have our moms or wives to clean up after us. Time to clean up after ourselves.

Last Group was a Jenga-style game with questions. It was a fun take on the game, but I don't recall now what the questions were.

When we got home, we hit the house chores up. Mike took off for sober living. Best wishes and prayers on your recovery, my man.

I found myself putting together new outdoor furniture with help from Jose. I got to find out he is a young father, and he was looking for guidance in life. He wanted to be more hands on with his children and doing stuff around the house. Speaking of that... It would be cool to have a job like George, the house maintenance man. He's kind of like the house dad.

I skipped workout, but I guess a day off isn't the worst thing in the world. A little rest and recoup time. We then took off for AA meeting at the park. All I know is that my feet are killing me. My toes are cracking in the webbing... Thought this crap would have gone away from not drinking.

Not too late to mention... Sarah from Ohio came over from West Hollywood. We now have two females in the house, but I think Angie's time is about through at the house. Losing Mama Bear again is going to suck.

Angie and I planned a quick supper. We did spaghetti and a salad. I put my twist on turning cheap sauce into a good one. Angie was quite impressed. Everyone has been appreciative of the cooking and family style dinners. All in all, it was a good end to a Monday that started on the wrong foot. God is good! Also, it is nice to be part of a group of clients that the staff says is the best they ever had. That we all work together and treat one another like family.

I ended the night creating a guitar lick for QP and Tre. Definitely going to get it recorded on video and sent to my phone. The music was sounding fire on the first take. I then went and talked with Chaz about house concerns and finished with some Xbox talk. Got to love the gamer community. I'm kind of interested to see how I play sober... that is, if I have the time to.

8-11-20: Tuesday: Sorting Things Out

I must be getting used to the time zone finally. I go to bed at like 11:30PM and wake up at 6:30AM. Probably should be hitting the hay a little earlier, but I always find myself dinking around or engaged in conversation. I did do a later (9:30PM) workout last night. My back has been on fire lately. I know there is hot weather coming, and not sure if the body is sensing it or what. I do know that I could go for a good chiro adjustment, and my inversion table, though.

Food sure is going fast. These young guys eat up everything and anything while they stay up all hours of the night. You'd think they were fifteen-year-old boys away from Mama. A quick fast forward past some monotonous stuff, and we are doing some Fighting Chance with Chad. He taught us some evasion tactics, and a punch/kick combo. Heck, if I ever get this back to work well, I just might try some kind of self-defense or boxing training.

We ended clinicals discussing the new house rules. Decisions were made that had everyone all pissy. They limited the garage use; in that they are creating more privacy for meds and phone use. You'd think that they had stolen these people's teddy bears and quit buying ice cream.

It remains a black and white area, and you can't let one and not the other. It really comes down to respect and common decency. I brought up the idea to temp a wall to create separation for phone calls and video calls, but I doubt they do it. It would make sense and that would never work.

I personally brought to attention Kristal's unprofessional work behavior and unsafe driving. She's got some screws loose on some bipolar aspects or something. Then she believes dancing while driving 80 in a 55 with seven lives in the fate of her hands is a grand idea. All in all, not a bad gal, just in my opinion, not really suited for the job.

It's either she is being buddy-buddy with the clients, snuggled up on a couch with them, and sluffing off meds, or she is on a power trip, super B, and causing a scene. All hail Kristal! I'm a tech, and you will respect my authority. Found out Nick from Phase 1 got a second chance, and is starting at the Phase 2 house.

We came home and I jumped straight on cooking prep. Creamy garlic chicken, potatoes with mini portabellas, peppers, onion and garlic, and California blend veggies with lemon pepper. Angie tried cutting off her finger, but was a trooper, and I started to get nervous on the sauce. Adam came out and was a hurting soul. These women out there can be ruthless. Guy is out here bettering his life, and this woman uses his absence as a weapon of destruction. Lord, I believe in your steadfast love, and that Adam's tears are all caught, and you will restore what is good.

The sauce wasn't thickening up, but started to around the 30-minute mark. In all my worries, the food ended up getting annihilated. The chicken and the sauce were a huge hit. The potatoes got destroyed, and everyone loved the lemon pepper on the veggie blend. In thinking the Lord was going to teach me it was okay to fail, I found out about preparation meeting opportunity.

We were even nice enough to let the techs in on the food and they were loving the home-cooked meals. We had last Group with Gabe. Dude cracks me up. He has a different sense of humor, but it has everyone in tears. This dude could be his own Netflix series... Not a bad idea, come to think of it. A series on the life in Phase 2 living of rehabilitation.

We talked about the struggles of re-entering the real world, and the triggers associated with it. My take is different; I must beat isolation, and create a life of exploring and living life outside of my apartment's walls. I had made it a prison cell, and trapped myself in my own mind. Living each day in fear and anxiety in a world I created to hate.

I'm still waiting on addiction counseling, when I'm going home, and receiving my short-term disability. I guess these are all things outside of my control. I know I have certain things set in place when I get home with AA. I am excited to find a sponsor and start working the steps. I talked with Dan and he said all my grievances are put on hold. I will put faith in the Lord on that targeting s**t show of a company.

8-12-2020: Wednesday: Grillin' and Chillin'

Morning started out as usual, other than Angie having stick-it notes. Mama Bear likes giving hugs, and posting positive vibes throughout the houses. I watched the weather... Weekend is going to be a scorcher in the valley... 105 degrees. First Group was with Kristal, and she actually stayed cool the whole time. I guess she broke her pinky in some fight with her friend and some random guy. It was said to be a "blood bath."

Our Monday meditation was on when we knew we had had enough. For early in the morning, people really opened up. Everyone but QP... He got kicked out of Group before it started, for sleeping. I got to give props to Kristal on that one. I do like techs that set that boundary.

Second Group was with Big Book Mike. Dude typically has a great meeting. I ended up getting pulled in to speak with Stefany. For once she/we were more productive, but still nothing on the addiction counseling side. Not real sure why that is being overlooked.

We talked about lining up a talk with my parents next Tuesday, and also Stefany talking to my kids one-on-one. I think they will open up to her more on the situation than to me. They want me to be happy and not worry. I know, though, that they are struggling with navigating life. My son has a chip on his shoulder and resentment towards his mom, it seems. Then again, he is a fifteen-year-old boy, but can definitely sense no structure and a sense of carelessness. But who am I to speak? Look where I am.

During lunch, I grabbed a few quick snacks, and then grabbed up an iPad. By this time, Kristal had a headache, and her job consisted of watching Netflix with "Her Boys." I ended up Facetiming my mother and daughter. Mama was over-happy to see my face. We lined up a talk time next Tuesday, and how long I may be staying. Even though I want to come home, Mama was all about staying.

Madison was cutting up potatoes. She wasn't psyched up about me possibly staying. She said she was the best psychologist in the U.S. and approved me coming home. Not real sure… I may try staying till the 26th of August. I would like to be back home for my daughter's birthday, but I guess I will let go and let God. He will decide what is best. **NO TURNING BACK!!** What I'm doing is for the best for my family and myself.

Beings it was Wednesday, we were done with groups. I went straight to pool, waiting on the food to be picked up for the BBQ party. When Adrian and Angie got back, it was game on! Ten racks of ribs… two men… Game Time! I ended up doing six racks. I never realized about pulling the membrane off on the back. Guess one learns something new every day.

Adam did more of a homemade rub, and did a covered, oven-baked rib. I did a Famous Dave's rub, threw them on the charcoal for a smoked flavor, and then foil-wrapped them. Adam went Sweet Baby Ray's, and I went Stubb's on BBQ sauce. Mike threw down a big-ass platter of mac 'n' cheese. His secret ingredient was cottage cheese. We did a salad, and Angie made corn bread. While we cooked, everyone else hopped in the pool.

Out of nowhere, Adrian and Todd pull up with Mary and Kris from Phase 1 house. I guess they were full so they pushed them our way. Business is business and I won't complain about having my Mary back in the picture. I guess they got rear-ended just shortly before arriving. Some van hauling a car smoked them from behind when they were stopped. Thankfully, no one was injured.

Food was served and we smashed it like a well-oiled family. It truly is great that we all can come together. God is good! After eating, Sarah (Ohio) kicked me off of doing dishes, so I decided to grill some more. Leftover meat from last week was about to go out of date, so I grilled it up. Twenty-four chicken legs and ten burgers later, and I moved backed to the kitchen. JC and Chris popped in.

I finished my cooking/prepping in the kitchen. I diced up both of the pineapples so that they would get eaten up. By this time, I finally sat down to relax for the day. I had drunk a Mountain Dew and realized there had been no caffeine for thirty-five days... That soda had me all jacked up. I got time to sit down and talk with Mary. It was nice getting to share a conversation with her again.

I came in to call Max quick, and he was chilling with my girl, Kat. He still wasn't back to work, but was doing good. Filled him in on the scoop, and then I headed back out to play some guitar. Everyone had taken off to somewhere. Angie swung through, and I guess they were all over playing cornhole. A part of me was going to read, and then people gravitated towards me. Tre came through and we did our song we had been working on. Sounding pretty dope.

The back was tight and the bodies dispersed. It was that time for a hot shower and bed. I drifted off to watching the second season of "The Ranch." That is one show I can actually watch. It always has me cracking up, and Mr. Kutcher is an Iowa native... Go, Hawks!

First off, it rained… That's right! Rain! I mean, it was maybe ten seconds and about twenty droplets, but it was raining in Hollywood, CA. I have decided to keep things short and sweet today. I need to get back into the groove of my schedule; not that being of service to others is a bad thing. I guess that, and the fact I'm not feeling it right this moment, either.

First Group was with Big Book Mike. His stories of living in New York, and trying to transition to Cali always crack me up. We played his game Zip, Zop, Zap, and Steve ended up winning. I couldn't get away from picking the guy not playing… dang rigged game, anyway. I also had a conversation with Tracey on how things were going. I can't say it was super beneficial.

Somehow in going home, I chose Phase 2, and now in wanting to go home, so I can be back for my daughter's birthday, I'm being told it is a 30-day program. I guess in all reality… What is another week on top of the time I have spent already? Part of me thinks that they know my insurance is good, and they will take it for every dollar they can.

We took lunch and I napped. We headed back for group with Steph, but she wasn't there. So we ended up watching the Amazon movie, "Beautiful Boy." It had Steve Carell from "The Office," and it was about a whole family struggle with a son that gets wrapped into drugs. Very good movie that I will have the kids watch. It really gives ya feels in the heart strings; for me especially, with a fifteen-year-old son.

We came back and Steph, Kris, and I hit the pool for like three hours. No more pale, white boy. This fatty has a golden tan. We did a Zoom meeting for last Group, which was fine by us all. We ended up just doing leftovers for supper. After dinner, we recognized Adam and Mike's sobriety. Mike had thirty days, and Adam had ninety. Proud of the men!

I got to talking with Chris from sober living. Him and JC had stopped in to visit. He showed me a video of him and Noah skydiving. I definitely want to do this thing with my kids. Hit that edge of the plane, and **NO TURNING BACK!!** Take that leap of faith!

I finished the night off talking to Gabe. You can tell this dude genuinely loves to help others out of their addiction. He takes the time to "unofficially" give you all of himself and his knowledge about recovery. It will be cool to talk to him, and to go in-depth on addiction counseling.

Two last things, well, three that came to mind as I Facetimed Madison. I explained to her about staying longer, and possibly not being home for her birthday. She was understanding, which was good. I also reached out to Amanda. I informed her about things, and me coming home. I knew this was a window to reconnect with my family. I just don't know what's all going down in conversation between her and my family members.

Live and let God! His will shall take me where I need to be. Lastly, that I recall, I was getting ... well, making some time to read the book that Edward gave me. So far, so good. There just happens to be a ton of typos, which I am sure he is aware of... I hope.

To end off the night, I went outside and hit a damn good pump on the weights. It must have been the influence of Gabe, and then Mike jumped in on shoulders. Gabe seemed scrawny but the dude was actually pretty jacked. The pump felt great even at 11:00PM.

8-14-2020: Friday: Cornhole

The heat had definitely settled in in the valley. It actually feels kind of humid… which sucks! Especially when it is 105 degrees.

After a small breakfast and a journal entry, I hit a quick work-out. Instead of hitting a shower, I just hopped in the pool to cool off before heading to clinicals. I found myself trapped in the bathroom, pissing with a monster cockroach. You don't see a lot of them, but the ones you do see are freaking enormous.

First Group was morning meditation with Mika. Tre and QP didn't make it to the start of the readings before falling asleep. Hell, Tre even brought a blanket to groups.

Other than those two, everyone participated. We spoke on repairing past damage. I haven't started step work, but I know this is something that will flow from my mind once I tap into it.

I grabbed a quick lunch and took a quick nap. 1:00AM to 6:00AM wasn't quite enough sleep for me last night. I drifted off to some native flute sounds.

As the day went on, the heat wasn't playing around. I totally forgot that after morning meditation, we had Darrell. For the most part, he was all over the place with his topic, like usual.

I stuck his ass when I commented on blueprints. I stated blueprints meant nothing if you don't know how to interpret them. He instantly tried to quiet me, but I meant it. The Big Book is just a book without a great sponsor to guide you. Like blueprints to construct a building are foreign to someone who has never seen them or built anything.

Third Group was with Tracey. We had to write down three things we cannot control that bother us. This was my list from class.

Things I Can't Control

1. Paying child support to a woman that uses it on her own selfish needs, and making me out to be the bad guy.
2. Management where I work, making unethical decisions to demoralize the company while trying to save their own faces
3. People putting on a fake mask, and then acting as if their lives are glamorous. Especially on social media… No authenticity!
4. Kids' mom wrapping my kids into screwing over the system, like it is a normal, moral way to exist.
5. In thinking my will without a spiritual foundation will create a life of peace and purpose.
6. That the parents in my extended family would take time to plan a reunion, instead of sitting back and just letting the connections fall apart into a Facebook-only family.
7. A falsified "Plan-demic" that has left this world an absolute s**t show. Controlling the masses with fear.
8. The damage done to my children in the depths of my addiction, including broken promises.

Tracey commended my list; in that it was a heavy one. I tend to carry a lot of the weight of the world on my shoulders, for what, at the time, seems like a good reason. I am learning, though, to pick my battles and attack accordingly. Everyone in their lists had some good stuff they wanted to work on, in letting go of control.

In trying to leave clinicals, the first group in the elevator found ourselves waiting a long period of time for the next group. The valet dude started running around, and the fire department rolled up. They ended up packing like twelve people in a six-man elevator, and it tripped the safety on it because it descended too quickly.

Talk about being happy I wasn't in that sh*t show. Twelve addicts trapped in an elevator that got up over 120 degrees, that was trapped between floors, and they couldn't get out. Sarah (OHIO) and I are both claustrophobic, and I would have lost my sh*t. Everyone ended up getting out safely. You could definitely tell the nerves were at an all-time high.

Adrian cancelled the park AA group, and we went straight for the pool. Mike P. and Chuck rolled in around 6PM to speak. It's always good to hear Mike speak. Hell, Chuck's story is a miracle as well. Could only imagine… He was pronounced dead three times, and he is still alive today, telling his story of overcoming addiction. I like when he said, "Trying to die didn't work, so I knew I had to try something else."

Chuck stayed and cooked with Brian L. on the grill. Kristal never ordered my Fat Sal's, so I guess maybe Sunday. Nothing was in it for her, so why would she? The laziest worker on this staff to date. Guess her job is to watch TV with Steve, and bitch when asked questions by clients.

Found out that Chuck actually did his Phase 2 at this house. I didn't realize he was an alumni. Adam brought up about doing a Zoom meeting with the Phase 1 people, once we leave. It will be cool to stay connected with all the people I had met here.

Mary and I escaped and got to talk under the gazebo for a good moment. Her eyes, smile, and accent just draw me in. I'm thinking I definitely could use another massage. Todd shot me with a water gun, and soon we had the gazebo full of people. Part of me, from the repairing damage detail, was thinking about writing letters again before going home. Especially ones for the kids… here soon.

I ended the night playing some cornhole. Jose and myself versus Sarah and Mike. They were up by eight, both games, and Jose would come out of nowhere. We took the win, both games. Sarah is pretty good. We go back and forth, cancelling each other's points. I was physically drained, like most the rest of the house. For some reason, Thursday night everyone had stayed up late.

8-15-2020: Saturday: Tensions Flare

S crew it! I'm diving right into the meat of this day. On top of a bunch of people who are sexually frustrated… It's hotter than Hell. The A/C at clinicals doesn't even come close to keeping up. Darrell done did went off the deep end today. I'm not sure what violations he all broke with clients, but HIPPA damn sure got left out of his thought process.

First John questioned him on a job, and he came out and said company was paying him $100.00 an hour. Ol' Miss said he was bragging about his material things at Phase 1, too. Then he went on to share personal information about a client who relapsed. Told family issues, and was stating names, and then it hit the fan.

Darrell asked Kris a question. Kris started to answer, and Darrell interrupted him, and tries to tell him how he should answer. Kris then calls him out, and states, "You ask me a question. Let me answer it!"

Anger grew quickly and Darrell started to get defensive. The whole vibe in the room went south. Darrell done did lost his mind. He was very unprofessional, and now he is floating in Kristal's boat. Mike was pissed off, too. Said he got so angry he had to walk away, because he wanted to knock Darrell upside his head.

Everyone went their own ways when we got home. I joined the pool party. I'm not into that Netflix binging, couch surfing agenda. We ended up having Sammy's cousin over, who was a barber, and we all got cuts. I went straight edge razor, full bald. There is a first time for everything. Pizza arrived, and it was time for the ultimate fights.

I don't watch that garbage, and it put me in a spot to start getting frustrated. The young guys in the back house don't pull their weight on chores. I ended up doing their dishes and mopped their floor. Not sure how they will make it in life on their own. They can barely wipe their own butts.

My frustration then transferred to Kristal. This gal clocked in to work, and only left the couch to feed her face. Meds didn't get handed out between 8-10PM, and all she had was an excuse. I took it upon myself to go straight into a workout. I knew I had to do something.

I wanted to lash out, but decided that wasn't best. I hit the exercise with great force. So hard that three others started walking, and later, Jose even jumped aboard. Accountability is huge with me, especially when it is made clear of my accountability. It seems they are hiring people that aren't mentally stable or just straight up lack professionalism.

When Chaz got back from grocery shopping, I pulled him aside. I had him get my CBD, and told him it appeared he was the only tech clocked in that was doing anything. He told me to pass my info on to Adrian.

Thank God for Mary... I hopped in the pool to cool off, and she was there to chat. Told me not to let it trigger me. She had a calming sense that returned me back to the ground. I finished off the night watching "Shameless" with her, and positioned myself perfectly for a shoulder massage. 2:00AM came quick and it was time for bed.

8-16-2020: Sunday: Tri-tip Sirloins

I slept in till 7:45AM, and that, my friends, will put a wrench in morning routines. I stayed up late and it's Sunday, so I decided, what the heck. I was actually looking forward to John's class. Some good ol' music therapy. The 12-step priest videos aren't too bad, either. The last two sessions, we went over steps 4 and 5. It will be interesting to actually go over them with a sponsor. Bradley said it like I called it… Once ya start writing on it, that all the memories start coming back.

I picked Casting Crowns's "Praise You in This Storm." It's one of my favorite songs by the group. Seemed like all the men had the feels for their women this morning. They say absence makes the heart grow fonder, and on this day that holds true. We heard a lot of slow R&B music… That was, until Sarah played some System of a Down.

Nothing gets a group going in the morning like the song "Violent Pornography." I'm sure Sarah has to have a softer side. I bet the gal needs some good true loving. She seems pretty angry at the world about something… Then again, I guess that was my thought process as well.

It got hot and we headed home. QP went to sober living today. Good dude and a funny one, but… put zero effort into his recovery, and he couldn't pick up after himself. I guess, in no spiritual revelation, and at his age, that he is too naïve to realize he is powerless. That or the system has him over-medicated to force a relapse. Which wouldn't surprise me, with the things you hear around the rooms.

I cooked lunch for Mary and myself. Scrambled eggs with spinach, sausage, peppers, and onions. I hit it with some Cajun seasoning and some hot sauce. No lie… it actually turned out really good. The sun was beaming down, and my sun-worshipping self was pool bound. This 105-degree stuff is warming up the pool

pretty quick. The water still feels good, but we got some green
algae stuff growing at an alarming pace.

I Facetimed the kids. Madison was eating dinner with her
mom's new boyfriend, and the boy was headed home from
Minnesota. He said he caught a couple more fish. I will see if they
let me check my phone tomorrow at clinicals on a break. I caught
Brian out front, washing the vehicles. I asked him if he cared if I
started the tri-tips on the charcoal. He insisted that I go for it.

I guess the tri-tip cut originated in California. They were pre-
seasoned, so I went straight to the grill with them. I smoked them
for a good thirty minutes, and then put them in a covered pan on
the gas grill at 300 degrees. Whatever this cut of meat was, and
how it was seasoned, was smelling and looking delicious.

Thank you, Lord, for tri-tip sirloin! Dinner was an explosion
of flavor in the mouth. Sarah did up some cheddar and garlic
mashed potatoes, and Angie made a portabella mushroom gravy.
The meat came out like a perfectly seasoned brisket. It was absolutely phenomenal. Kristal asked if I could teach her my ways, and
said she was blown away when I told her I never cooked on charcoal until I came to Phase 2.

Other than Kris and I whooping Sarah and Mike 4-0 in cornhole, and Chaz doing a gas station run so I could get some elec-
trolytes… I was moving slow. I did end up mopping the floor,
reading some of Edward's book, and watched some YouTube with
Bradley. He is leaving back for home on Tuesday.

8-17-2020: Monday: Flu bugs and flirtin'

Woke up to Montezuma's Revenge. Brian L, Tre, and Angie were all throwing up out both ends. The day before, it was Sarah and Adam. It seems like it is just a 24-hour bug, but I started pumping vitamin C. They got it… might as well take it. On top of that, I have been taking my vitamin B complex. So far, so good, and prayers to those who have it, on a speedy recovery.

Adrian did hook up the house. He picked up a bunch of chicken noodle soup, crackers, and Emergen-C. I'm pretty sure that most everyone has been exposed. I should probably pop some melatonin, and get me some good sleep in the coming nights. I did give Angie a big hug. I have always been one to take colds from my kids. I don't like seeing people suffer. I made dang sure to keep the sick people by the door in the van. I wasn't about to get ralphed on.

Clinicals are miserable! It's hot and they just suck to sit through. I don't recall morning meditation, but I do know that second Group was with Tracey. Bradley read his timeline, and it went deep. There wasn't a dry eye in the room. Props to him for digging that deep, and powering through all the emotional traumas in his life. He is to leave tomorrow, and he has definitely left an impact on me. The guy is an inspiration, and he will definitely be missed. Good ol' Brett Favre.

After lunch, we came back to Breath Work with Sam. I ate too much and shouldn't have popped that CBD. Instead of mind tripping, I just flat out fell asleep. Note to self… not a good idea to do those two things before a deep breathing session. I'm sure I was snoring good and loud.

After Breath Work, we had PsychoEd with Don. I'm not exactly sure how to take this guy yet. He didn't come last weekend, and this week came and still wasn't prepared. Part of me says he failed at what he tried to accomplish in psychology, and then he settled for whatever job he could land. He does have some great material, but it just seems disconnected and unorganized.

We came home and couldn't swim because the pool got shocked. I quickly started thinking what I could cook up. Mary came to me a little upset. After I called out Nick and Kristal, now all the sudden, Mary is being too flirtatious with me. Why they went at Mary was and is stupid. The retaliation was supposed to be directed at me, but just made them look dumber. They didn't want to battle with me in person.

We both went inside and did some dinner prepping. Mary was throwing down a lemon curry chicken. I decided to prep beef and chicken tacos. Dinner was a little late, but was it ever a feast. I had never eaten lemon curry before. Curry has a very distinct taste. My chicken tacos came out fire as well. I smoked the thighs before finishing them off on the stove top. Mary and I shared a small street style taco, and it was delicious.

I'm going to blame flip-flops on why Kris was sucking it up on bags. Sarah was on fire. We ended up losing 3 games to 1, but we did end the night on a win. We ended up getting Joe and Cliff in. Big Joe is pretty seasoned on the ol' gitfiddle, and he also has an awesome voice. Cliff is an OG that can spit some truth. Not a bad addition to the house, in both men.

8-18-2020: Tuesday: Free T-shirt

Just starting to write this on the 20th of August. I want to say, screw it, but I got laundry in the dryer, Mountain Dew in my veins (cheat day... my bad), and its 12:30AM. Sometimes you have to burn both ends of the candle. Anyways... I got a small workout in before heading to clinicals for the day. The back was actually feeling pretty decent, and made for an enjoyable workout.

I got the chance to let the parents in on a counseling session with Stefany. It went pretty much exactly how I expected. I got to get out that it killed me to be part of a broken family. Especially in being in a broken family with my kiddos. Mom blabbed on the whole time and took zero fault in my brother leaving the family.

Stefany wondered why I didn't call my parents out. I knew it wasn't the time, and I also wanted to keep the call cordial and informative. That and I don't think that that is a trigger. I didn't like the brokenness, but it wasn't really my battle.

I missed Saeed during my meeting and that sucks. I love this dude. He gets all hyped up and blurts out craziness. We have been quoting him while we played bags. If anybody sank a bag, Mike and I would yell out, "You are successful!! Yes, and Yes, True and True!!"

I did a small lunch in prepping for an outdoor workout with Chad and Fighting Chance. Luckily, we only had six people, so we worked out inside. It was 115 degrees, and if we weren't inside, we were outside on the seventh floor roof. Screw all that!

Unfortunately, the A/C was jacked, and we still sweated our balls off. Chad pushed us hard at the end. I had to have over 200 push-ups on the day. I'm sure this one will leave the body sore. There was a guy fixing the A/C, so hopefully tomorrow is better.

After Group with Chad, my shirt was absolutely soaked in sweat. I used my wits to pull off getting a Hollywood ATC T-shirt. Confessed I couldn't sit for an hour in a soaked shirt, and that I would return it before I left... NOT! When I got home, I whipped up my taco stuff from the night before. Big Joe was playing guitar and singing. I guess the dude plays by ear. "Lord, please lead me to my singing voice!"

We had our last meeting with Gabe. I always enjoy his groups. As expected, the group went extremely well, and the one thing I needed to work on was integrity... which makes sense. There was a Doritos wrapper sitting outside that I was fighting myself about picking up and I didn't. In leading by example, it didn't matter who did it. I shouldn't have got angered in fighting myself to pick it up. I just need to lead by example and pick the dang thing up.

To end the night, Kris and I won 2 out of 3 games on cornhole. I had to carry the weight, but a win is a win. I carried on my nightcap by speaking with Chaz and Gabe. Both these guys are great dudes that give you all of themselves to give you a better chance at recovery.

We talked about me getting home for my daughter's birthday, personalities at the house, and Chaz spoke me up about the work I was putting in on my recovery. He told me I will never know the impact I created at the house. All I can say is that I am proud to be part of the greatest recovery group they have had come through the program.

8-19-2020: Wednesday: Get rid of the Allergy

I woke up late again, and, boy, was I sore from push-ups. Ol' Chad put the hurt on me yesterday in just a short period of time. We came to find out that the van wasn't broke, the steering wheel was just locked. Hopefully, Kristal didn't figure that out because that would be a real blow below the belt to Chaz.

Kristal was a shining star this morning. She came forward with her Super "B" cape on this morning for morning meditation. For some unknown reason she is always taking notes, and tells people they will be marked as noncompliant if they don't share. Just so happens, she is the only facilitator doing this.

I wanted to talk to Reno about going home because I guess Cheryl had nothing to do with it, or at least that's what I was told. He ended up going to West Hollywood when Jose left. I was scheduled for a meeting with Tracey from 1-2, but on Wednesdays we get done at 11:30AM. Not sure what Einstein planned out meetings. It doesn't cease to amaze me that the schedule is always messed up, communication is always broken, and no one is on the same page. Way to go, Reno!

Group was with Big Book Mike, and it was a better one. Dude is hilarious and straightforward, but he respects the client and does his best to give his interpretation of the Big Book. I brought up the word, "Allergy," and how it had been on my mind that it had made no sense to me.

Eat peanuts: get hives, itch, eyes swell, and can't breathe... Drink beer: relax, numbs pain, allows me to function... It's a chemical alteration that is happening but its feel-good until it becomes a dependency, but that still isn't an allergy.

Big Book Mike brought up that when you drink, it is how it creates cravings, and the craving is the allergy. My rebuttal, addict is to addiction... addicted is to craving to stabilize the absence of a dependency of substance, not an allergic reaction to alcohol/substance.

You can't take Benadryl and drink more. If you have an allergic reaction, you stop and seek medical help. In end stages, alcoholics have to keep putting it into the system to function without withdrawal symptoms. Mike came back with, "You are right! Allergy sucks in this book. Just get rid of that word!"

We came back home, and I was straight in the pool. Nothing better than the rays beating down on the body at high noon. I didn't get this beautiful bronze skin in the shade. Plus, at noon it doesn't matter what direction you float. Then I realized I screwed up. I saw Kristal... I thought she was driving to the beach, so I stayed home. Just my luck, Mika drove, and I was stuck with her... but... **NO TURNING BACK!!**

It worked out, though, for the best. I was able to contact my mother and Amanda about coming home on the 26th of August. I was going to be able to be home for my daughter's birthday. I also got to feel how soft Mary's skin was. One could say we were flirting in the pool. She was right, when it was brought up, that it just makes you want to do it more.

About three hours later and the beach crew stumbled back in. My toes were cracking from being in the water too long. We ended up getting a new girl from Phase 1. Her name was Megan. I didn't really talk to her much, but heard she was moved after seven days.

After drying off, I hit the charcoal grill up, and commenced in cooking up chicken for Angie's Alfredo supper, inspired by JoJo. Right as supper was being served, Chaz decided it was a good time to go to the gas station. I made up two plates for us before taking off. I know how these vultures work when the food hits the table. Just as expected, the food was demolished when we got back. Luckily, I did right in setting food aside. Once again, supper was delicious.

The main group gravitated towards the cornhole boards, and needless to say, I opened a can of whoop ass. Ol' Miss (Kris) and I went 5-0. Kris started throwing like me (spinning the bag), and you could tell he was gaining more control. Joe better find himself a good partner because Kris and I are becoming a force to be reckoned with.

Everyone took off but Mary, Tre, and myself. I have been casually flirting all day. More or less just rubbing up on her to let her know my presence. Seems like, for whatever reason, though, that we can never get alone. God is saying, "You aint here to hook up, ol' son!"

Ended up spitting some wisdom to Tre about getting clean and chasing his dreams. Hopefully, it sticks with the kid. He has been better ever since QP left. Much more awake and participating. I finished the night doing laundry and writing my 8-18 entry in my journal. The dryer went off around 1:00AM. I folded up my clothes and called it a night.

S o, I am slacking big time on this journaling thing, but I am realizing that I need to focus. I get involved in socializing and having fun, and it gets so late, and then I reach a point of exhaustion for the day. The writing at that time ends up getting pushed to the next day.

All in all, I had become a prisoner of my apartment and isolated myself from all life. For the first time in quite some time, I was actually enjoying myself and the company of others. There was a life outside the walls of my broken mind. There was actually good in the world.

Adrian led first Group, and, boy, did he get the feels going early in the morning. Our topic was dealing with the loss of a loved one in sobriety, and pulling through without relapsing.

This was something that hit me hard, even though I didn't get the chance to share. I know my father's health isn't the greatest, and if I lost him in the depths of my addiction... who knows where I would have turned in my depression. I think it would have been the nail in the coffin, or whatever they say.

Now, with over forty days of sobriety, and a group of support, I feel that I am creating the tools to help navigate life on life's terms. Finding ways to reach out and also alleviate stresses of life. Alcohol... my best friend, was the only thing I ever knew, and it was killing me.

Big Book Mike rolled in with a fun-filled day. We started with his game, "Zip, Zop, Zap." Like Mike says... it's a stupid game, but it's fun and challenging. We then went to, "One-Word Sentence." What seems to be simple ends up throwing people completely off, in trying to compose a sentence that makes sense.

Typically, by the fourth word, the sentence turned sexual or to drugs... imagine that in a room full of addicts. Every once in a while, though, we would pull off a good sentence. Last we did improv, and I got paired with Ol' Miss (Kris). We were given the topic of taco truck, and I couldn't help but go straight into, "Hey! Smell this..."

I ended up meeting with Tracey, and he is trying to make me stay till the 29th. It doesn't really make sense when he is saying sixty days. My sixty days aint till September 6th. I'm just trying to get home and surprise my daughter for her fourteenth birthday. I will have thirty days at Phase 2 on the 29th, but as for what Tracey is talking about... His math sucks.

We then had Group with Steph. We did a writing exercise on past, present, and future. I hope I can get it back. It was an awesome writing exercise. As usual, whenever I got some good stuff rolling, I don't get the chance to share, but it's all good.

We then coined out Angie and Steve. They were both headed for sober living. Steve's presence will be missed, in holding down the couch. Only place I ever saw the guy. Mama Bear, on the other hand, is going to suck to lose. She is a huge part in keeping the house going.

We came home and I made flatbread pizzas as an appetizer/snack. Chicken, bacon, oregano, jalapeno, red onion, garlic, spinach, and mozzarella with an Alfredo/ranch white sauce. Let's just say I could have made five more. It got demolished. Starting to think that Kristal is hating the fact that she likes me, but we will leave that for what it is. She is like my little redheaded stepsister.

I ended up hitting the pool until Group at 7:30PM. Cliff, Sarah, and Mary ended up cooking dinner. I personally skipped supper and did a workout. It was much needed, and I got an awesome sweat going. I had been feeling pretty stressed and it definitely worked as a release tactic. I swapped clothes and joined Adam, Mike, Sarah, Mary, and Kris by the pool. Kris and Mike were dogging on Darrell's egotistical-being. We are all hoping to see a change in him come tomorrow. See if he was humbled from last week.

We made our way over to the bags arena. Kris and I smoked Sarah and Mike. I grabbed a victory bowl of ice cream. Tell you what… it hit the spot! I then conversed with Adam and Mary, and made my way to the gazebo.

I waited on Mary, but she left me hanging. I went to bed around 1:30 AM. I fell asleep waiting on her. It was a beautiful night, there was no humidity, and a nice breeze from the ceiling fan.

8-21-2020 Friday: A kiss goodnight

The good Lord must have understood our frustrations because Darrell's demeanor had completely changed. Mike, being all pissed off, and Darrell was actually on his side. Group actually turned out pretty good.

We talked on healthy/unhealthy fears. I didn't get to share, like normal. Some reason, Darrell always skips me. There is always tomorrow, though. Maybe one day I will get the chance to tell my story, like my mom had mentioned before I got on the plane.

Just my luck, Reno never showed up, but I brought up going home to Adrian. It never ceases to amaze me, the run around. After lunch, we came back and coined out Adam. Strange God-moment... Bradley showed back up and he didn't even know Adam was getting coined out.

We took a brief break, and I got the chance to talk to Tracey. I brought up the sixty days thing that he was trying to push. He instantly switched to sending me home. I get to surprise Madison now!!!

Adam did his timeline. What a story this man has. It is a true testimony of how messed up the U.S. government leaves its soldiers after war. It was cool that Roxy showed up, and that Bradley had stopped in. Bradley always had positive and powerful things to say, and you could feel every word he spoke.

I hit the pool when we got home, even though the clouds came in. Mary came and chilled along with Joe. Tre came out stunting some crazy-looking Versace shirt and white jeans. No job, but somehow has money to stunt.

I guess this is where they talk about saving face over rear end. More worried about his looks than his problems with drugs. To be a kid again, I guess... Hell, I can't afford to pay attention, but... **NO TURNING BACK!** I'm gaining more clarity each and every day.

We hit the AA at the park. The meeting drug on, but the

weather was decent, and the main speaker was cool. A true blue-collar worker that found meaning in a sober life. On the way home, Mary brought up what I thought of our relationship. Not sure if it was what she wanted to hear, but I told her I wanted to keep things organic, and let what happens happen.

We came home and whipped up a spicy pasta that I had envisioned in my head. Groceries were pretty minimal, so I was scrapping for a quick meal to throw together. Mary learned really quick that I don't mess around in the kitchen, but I also haven't had any complaints yet. Meal turned out awesome, paired with some hot dog bun garlic bread. People seemed really impressed and I got a bunch of compliments.

I ended up working my way to the gazebo after a late supper. I had to get away from the new chick, Megan. Wack job, pathological liar, and she liked getting touchy-feely and I wasn't having it. You could tell this girl was yearning for love and acceptance and struggling with co-dependency. Not this guy!

Mary didn't leave me hanging tonight. We stayed up late, talking about life and real feels with being sober. The next thing you know... we were lip-locked! I felt fourteen again... scared, nervous, excited. I don't recall the last time kissing a gal for the first time, being sober. One kiss turned into many as we made our way to bed.

One thing I expressed was I didn't want to make things weird. With a heart full of butterflies, we embraced once more and kissed one last time. Talk about feeling alive! I headed for a shower and sleep. Let's see what tomorrow has in store.

8-22-2022: Saturday: Just What I Expected

Woke up with a little time before clinicals, so I took time to get a quick pump in. I think I have been staying up too late. My body isn't seeming to recover; that or another front is moving in. Probably staying up late kissing on Mary...

We had our first group with Darrell, and it was another good one. It seems that our words as clients were taken well, and he adjusted properly. I talked about letting my heart go again, and having walls built up from past destruction.

Everything was going well and then Kristal entered our presence. She brought a threatening attitude, and she got fifteen negative energies back. I tipped it off by saying I had a right in my life, off of the reading, and I choose to be non-compliant. I left the room to talk to Adrian, and I guess the whole room followed my lead and they all went in on her.

I thought I had my anger out, but it instantly came back when I re-entered the room. I let go and spoke my mind as a pissed-off client that wouldn't be bullied or threatened. I told her she could shove her non-compliance crap up her a**, and that it didn't mean squat.

Also, that she was getting paid and that we had a choice to not put up with her as clients, and that we could determine her losing her job. She then started crying, as if attacked. Well, that's what ya get! Come attack us and it's 1 on 15. Hopefully, it was a lesson in humility, and she was humbled.

Adrian ended up coming in and we put her on blast for her threatening demeanor. It was a long time coming, with how she slacked around the house, and how she power-tripped on people all the time. We then went back to the compound, and I got some pool time in before the party. The girls took off shopping with Adrian.

Seemed like I was always left out of doing cool things. Clients got haircuts, went shoe shopping and stuff. Hey, Jeff!... Can you put this together and maybe we might get ya something to eat? I guess it is what it is. I'm just not sure how to ask or whatever... heck, I wasn't informed we were able to do these things.

Phase 1 showed up with a gang of meat again. I manned the grills so Big Joe could spend time with his girl from Washington. Everything was going well until I caught the grill on fire. It burned itself out, but it got a little hairy there for a brief moment.

It was nice seeing some old faces from Phase 1, especially Edward and Ty. Adam and Angie also swung in. Got to say, God blessed me with an awesome group of recovering addicts. We have turned into quite the family. I wish everyone the best in their recoveries and new lives in sobriety.

When Phase 1 left, I transferred two huge spare rib racks to slow-cook in the oven. I hit some bags with Kris, Mike, and Sarah. Once again, Kris and I put the hurting on these folks. We became a force to be reckoned with on the bags arena. After the butt-whooping, I made up a BBQ sauce. I coated the ribs and put them back in to caramelize while I strummed the guitar.

Mary approached me, and I could already tell it was "a talk." I figured the kiss led to some emotional reaction. She said she felt as if she was chasing me, when I was just busy all day. I guess I was running from her, and then taking some time to myself to decompress was the icing on the cake.

I told her I needed to stick to my routine because the reality of going home was drawing near. It was a must that I stayed focused on my recovery, not just for me, but also for my children. It actually felt good to share my feelings sober and in control. I didn't come here to hook up, and will be damned if I'm made out to be the bad guy in someone else's selfishness,

I got a chance to talk with Shawn (Hollywood). Man has a brilliant mind, and all in all, a very kind soul. Dude is a phenomenal musician, and we actually share a lot in common. He, too, suffered from alcoholism, but he was from Encino area. We talked on life, guitar, God, and our disease. I will definitely be in contact with this guy after leaving. Reminds me a lot of my old best friend, Kevin.

Ribs were done and they were on point. Tender and juicy, gleaming with a sticky, caramelized BBQ sauce. I mixed a Smokey Mesquite, Hawaiian, and habanero BBQ sauce with apple cider vinegar, Dijon mustard, and a red wine vinaigrette. Whatever I did... It worked and the house loved and demolished them. To think, Steph and Mary thought they were bad because they smelled funny.

I finished the night talking about life and the son I have never met. It was a good decompression to the night. Ol' Chaz is always up to listen and give great advice. I did my journal entry and hit the hay after a long day.

8-23-2020: Sunday: Mama Mia… Garlic!

Woke up at a decent time and pushed myself to work out. I started off lethargic, but I ended up getting a good pump in. Feels good to get the blood flowing, first thing in the morning. This will definitely need to stay in my routine, to keep my body feeling well. I had started the journey right out of divorce with a personal trainer, but alcohol said, "Hey, Jeff! I'm way easier and I numb."

Got to clinicals and John didn't show. Adrian stepped in to save the day so we could still play our song for the day. My song choice was the acoustic cover of "Face Down," by The Red Jumpsuit Apparatus. I chose this song because my kids' mother went through an abusive relationship, and my daughter and I cover it when we jam. It made me think about her, with her birthday approaching.

Second Group was also with Adrian. We divided into groups by age. Forties, thirties, and then twenties and younger. We did a lifeboat exercise. It was a list of twelve people, and you could only keep six. Each person had a good and a bad trait. It was a fun little exercise to see how people thought.

We had four guys and one girl in our group. We tried bringing the 22-year-old go-go dancer with fake breasts on the boat, but Sarah talked some sense into us men… boys… I guess fake breasts aren't necessary for survival. I thought it was a great idea to keep the morale up in a boat full of dudes, but what do I know?

When we got home from clinicals, I went on a cleaning rampage. I figured after the flu bug had hit that it wouldn't be a bad idea to deep clean. I cleaned the bathrooms and mopped the bedroom floor. Afterwards, I moved to the kitchen. Sarah was preparing lasagna with a homemade meat sauce, so I just cleaned up behind her.

As usual, all three trashes were full, and people just kept cramming more trash into them. It was like living in a house full of teenagers. People can be nasty and lazy. I feel so sorry for these men's wives, girlfriends, and moms. These men will live in straight-up filth and not bat an eye.

After a little swimming, Mary and I talked again. She admitted to being selfish, and that she needed to respect my decisions. Also realizing she also needed to focus on herself, and not trying to figure me out. Cheryl told her to steer clear of relationships. Sean ended up coming through with the guitar. He broke out of his shell and sang while playing. HOLLYWOOD!!!!! Absolute star!

Supper was done, and was it ever so amazing. Homemade Italian food is no joke. The lasagna and garlic bread were to die for. After supper, Chaz, Sarah, and I went grocery shopping for the house... I finally got to go somewhere... YAY!!!

Let's just say the grocery store didn't have a shortage of beautiful women. It was short, though, on canned chicken. I ended up getting a Monster Zero. It was my first time drinking one since I left Iowa. Let's just say it had me bouncing off the walls. Whatever it did, though, it mixed with the garlic and my stomach went on the fritz. I thought I needed Depends to get out the store.

After we got all the groceries home and packed away, I grabbed up the guitar, and chilled in the garage with Chaz and Noah. I was too wound for sound, off the caffeine. I guess not the best idea at 10PM, but Chaz was buying so I gave in. Dang, the drink was good. Just the carbonation was refreshing on the taste buds. The night tech ended up not showing and Kristal came back in at like 2AM. With her arrival, I thought it's time for bed.

First Group with Noah got a little weird today. It normally doesn't go religious, but something about the morning meditation went that way. I talked on my relation with God, and how when I first accepted Jesus as my savior, that I never got to know him.

I didn't have a relationship with a higher power or seek to do his will. It's crazy how quick we blame God when things go bad, but praise ourself when things are going good and right. All the good in my life, I credited to myself for being awesome. What ignorance... I was never thankful or grateful.

I then met up with Tracey about the plane ticket home. $530.00 one way to Cedar Rapids, Iowa. He did find a $230.00 one to Des Moines, but Dad said Cedar Rapids, and he didn't care what the price was.

Second Group was with Tracey, and we ended up coining out John. Todd was supposed to get coined out, but he refused. Stubborn ol' fart. Anyway... my coin would be coming soon. Kind of wondering if Tracey will have me do a timeline or what.

I saw Cheryl in the kitchen area of clinicals and she, more or less, blew me off. Gave me a weird feeling that just added to my experience with the clinical staff. I never really connected to anyone, and I seemed to get blown off by everyone when it came to them being accountable.

I never went in-depth on anything, and anything I asked for was forgotten or pushed off to a later day. Is what it is... I'm not in control of this experience, but, more or less, here to regain my own life. **NO TURNING BACK!** I guess I will just lean on the techs that I get along with.

Came back to clinicals and Mary and myself were once again holding hands in the back seat of the van. We get our teenage flirting in where we can. We came back to Sam and my last Breath Work.

I let Mary in on my secret to escape the mind, and how I had had out-of-body experiences. Mary had a good session. I relaxed, but that was about it. For some reason, I tossed and turned. Probably because I am anxious to get home and hug my kids and parents. I left Sam with a hug and put her on to the band Needtobreathe.

Next Group was PyschoEd with Don. Talk went to cell phones and media controlling the masses. I fear for my children, along with all children, on this topic. The smartphone is a very powerful thing. In a sense, it does its best at playing God.

The problem is the ease of manipulation and casting fear upon the populations. Especially the ignorant and naïve, and I, too, have been this person. We also talked on the effect of substance abuse on kids wanting instant satisfaction. That without the pouring in of "likes," that they feel their lives are meaningless. This will be an interesting problem over the next ten years.

And... this is where I got involved and don't remember much. I held hands with Mary again on the way home. I do remember prepping fajitas for Tuesday's last meal, but past that I draw completely blank.

Oh, wait... I almost forgot Fat Sal's. I finally got it from Gavin. He got me the Fat Texas. All I can say is, Google it. It is a whole meal on one bun kind of sandwich. I do remember chillin' in the pool, and cuddling with Mary and talking life. Sarah was talking with Mike, and everyone else disappeared.

I ended up eating half of the grease-bomb and called it quits. We ended the night with a group movie night. Threw on a Rob Zombie movie, and I cuddled under a blanket with Mary. Man, is her skin soft... We slowly got up, and we got some alone time where we got to sneak in some kisses before we heard somebody approaching.

It was weird... anyone and everyone could be making out in the kitchen, but for some reason I was being hawked. The techs followed Mary and I where ever we went. Heck they were even going in and checking Mary's bedroom while she slept. If it wasn't for being here in rehab though... there would definitely have been some all-nighters.

I knew my time was coming to an end and boy was it ever bittersweet. While anxious to get back home... there was also a sense of security in the group. We had become a family, and I know right now I will miss them all like crazy. At times it all has seemed completely unreal. As if I am in some kind of weird dream, and then I will wake up back on my couch in my apartment.

8-25-2020: Tuesday: Fajitas for the Win!

I t all became a blur, but I was lucky enough that God led me to write down a couple notes of how the day went. I started off the day holding hands with Mary on the way to clinicals. Right as we started to grow in our relationship, and it was time for departure. Going to miss her beautiful face and pretty accent.

Morning meditation was with Noah. We spoke on breaking free from chains that held us captive to the disease of addiction. We don't realize how much we operate in fear. It used to paralyze me, but now it motivates me. I had a false sense of security while desperately alone, and a place I never want to revisit.

I called Mama and there was no word on the plane ticket yet. We then had Group with Saaed. This dude continues to crack me up. I don't recall it all, but in my notes, I got one of his best sayings,

"If you are hungry and lick the door… No one is going to give you a hot dog!"

I know I got coined out after lunch and everyone put their word in my coin, but in a way, it sucked, because all the people I really bonded with and knew me were gone. All the newcomers didn't really get a chance to know me or my story. I guess, in that aspect, I didn't get all emotional. I actually showed strength and gave words of encouragement to all those newer to the program.

At the end of groups, I got the news on my flight. The direct flight to Cedar Rapids had changed to me waking up at 4:30AM to leave home at 7:00AM. Whelp… Guess I am doing goodbyes tonight.

I spent my last day doing what I do best. I hit that kitchen, well, actually both kitchens, up. I had prepped chicken, steak, and shrimp fajitas. They occupied two huge aluminum foil pans. I ended up using the stoves in both houses to pull it off, and, boy, did I ever pull it off. Had to be the best meal I have ever cooked in my life. Praise be to God!

I don't recall a whole lot of the rest of the night other than hugs and handshakes with clients and techs. I do however remember talking with Mary, and she said that she would wake up with me to see me off. I could sense her sadness and the puppy love that had evolved would be missed.

I went to my room and packed up all my things. I came with one small suitcase half-full, and now go to leave with two big handbags and a suitcase with a zipper that is about ready to bust. I didn't try to acquire too much, but all my journaling and writings are a bag in itself.

I awoke to my alarm to shut it off as quick as possible so that I didn't wake any of the others. I gathered up my things and took them to the front door. I finally got my cell phone back so that I could be in contact with the Uber. Heck, I even had my wallet back.

My heart was beating uncontrollably. So excited to leave but sad in leaving. I hated flying but I think I was past that. I wasn't sure that Mary had set her alarm, but she did. I gathered up the rest of my stuff from the staff member and awaited the Uber with Mary.

As the car drew nearer, Mary and I stepped outside. What better way to end this movie in my life. Once overlooking the skyline of Los Angeles, California and the Hollywood sign... Now wrapped up in the arms of this beautiful woman. Lip-locked for the last time. It seemed like a cliché ending, but I will take it.

We hugged one last time as the car pulled in the driveway and the staff came to get me. ADIOS!!! As I rode in the back seat of the Uber, so many memories flew through my mind. Smiles and tears... I did it! I stuck through it all and came out stronger. Now on to the next chapter.

I don't really recall much of the flight, but I do know I was ready to land. My parents awaited my return at the airport. The Christmas gift I got them the year before was a shirt with my face plastered all over it... sure enough, they were wearing them. Tears of joy cast over all our faces as we embraced in hugs. I was back... Iowa soil...

I don't recall all the stories that were shared but I am sure I talked my parents' ears off. What I do remember, though, was the anxieties that hit when my parents wanted to do Mexican food. This was my last time drinking before I left.

Not even an hour onto native soil and the tests already began. God had my back. The only place that ended up being open was

Hardee's. My heart was racing at the thought of Mexican. How was I going to be able to watch others partake in drinking? That was the one safety net in California.

To end the day, I remember driving to the gas station by myself. That same gas station that my truck had been stuck on autopilot to, for the last three years. Once again, the nerves flared up and fear set in. It's crazy... I went in, grabbed a Dew and a gallon of milk, and I made my way out the store.

As I climbed in my truck, I had tears fill my eyes. For the first time in years, I walked right past the alcohol with no urge. I had a smile from ear to ear. Thank you, Lord! What seems such an easy task held much power. The one thing about alcohol is it is everywhere and so socially accepted.

10-9-2022: Sunday: Finished It!

Well, I woke up at 5:00AM. Work has been kicking my butt, so I zonked out at about 7:30PM on the couch from the night before. I took a hot shower and sat down to put a cap on this thing. What was supposed to be a thing I typed up as soon as I got home turned into a two-year process.

As I recapped these last days, I couldn't help but fall into the emotions of the moment. 5:30 AM on a Sunday morning and I'm sitting at my kitchen table crying over my laptop. Tears of joy and sadness of the departure.

One could say a lot has changed. I used to stay up till 5:30AM, battling my demons and trying to drown myself on dry land. Now I'm wide awake and excited to be getting to go to church, and this is where the next chapter starts for you, the reader.

My life over the last two years has been nothing short of a miracle, in many ways. In surrendering my will over to God's will once I returned home, now my life has radically changed. I got into a church and found out I had an anointing over my life to share my story of being **Beyond Broken**.

The following pages of this book is a recap of my first two years in sobriety and key points in the building of my spiritual foundation. The ups and the downs, but living life on life's term… One Day at A Time! In God's will for my life.

PART II
BEYOND BROKEN

REDEEMED, RESTORED, AND RENEWED

BEYOND BROKEN

Just when I thought remembering the first ten days of my sobriety was a daunting task... and here I sit, trying to remember the last two years. Then add a brain injury (tell y'all about that one later) ... but thanks to Facebook, I have a decent timeline to work with. I encourage you, the reader, to sit back, relax, grab a snack and a drink, and get ready for the ride. **BEYOND BROKEN!** A journey that began with a broken man wanting to end his time in this world, to later find himself being redeemed, restored, and renewed through Jesus Christ. This is my testimony.

A little recap from the beginning of this story... I had kids out of wedlock at a young age. That relationship went south, and I spent years destroying myself, and feeling like a total failure as a father. In my mid-twenties, I accepted Christ into my life. I actually had what one would call a "burning bush" experience, like the way God got Moses's attention in the Bible.

It was the first time in my life that I encountered the Holy Spirit in that way. They did an altar call at the end of a church service, and I felt fire run through my body. It was as if something out of this world raised my hand up. I opened my eyes and the preacher locked eyes with me. He then started talking to me as if he had followed me around for the last ten years. Yet I had never spoken to this man before in my life beyond a "Hello" when I came into church.

Although it was such a powerful experience, I took this moment for granted. Something that would later humble me to my knees. Many blessings poured into my life. I met my soon-to-be wife, and got 50/50 custody of my kids. My life was on fire. Anything I touched turned to gold, and my pride and ego gave no thanks to my Creator.

I had a beautiful wedding on the beaches of Florida, swam with dolphins, and all that good stuff. I became a volunteer fire-fighter, and I also started a nonprofit. I was at an all-time high. I had accepted Christ, but thought that everything that was happening in my life was from my own self-will. Man was I about to get rocked.

The wife and I pulled away from church at the same time we went to get full custody of my children. I was working long hours and was beyond maxed out for my schedule. It's often in times and situations like ours that our pasts come to haunt us. In my mind, we were both broken people that had suppressed our traumas.

Our walls went up fast and we were both on a path to destruction, and hell-bent on destroying one another in that process. For the most part, I had my drinking at bay, except for the occasional weekend drunk fest. It soon became an every-night ordeal in which I kept trying to hide my usage. Alcohol was my best friend... Hell, at that time, it was my only friend other than the dog.

It seemed like I was supposed to go to work as much as I could, smile for pictures, and not have any say in the family, but be the one to fix all the problems. I tried to be present, but I turned to isolating and destroying myself. They say the road to Hell is paved with good intentions. From being on a high in life to feeling completely decimated.

I ended up having a court battle for custody of the kids. The kids' mom slapped her boyfriend on the way out, and my lawyer destroyed everyone he called to the stand. We thought we had won full custody of my kids.

After a few short days, not even enough to read all the information we had, the judge ruled that nothing had changed. My first thought was, *WTH!!! You have got to be f***king kidding me!.* Over two years and a good $50-60 thousand bucks down the drain. Talk about knocking the wind out of a guy's sails. I was angry, tired, broke, without love... Then it all spiraled out of control.

Things became physically and verbally abusive in our marriage. Divorce was right around the corner. What was once a breath of fresh air had turned into the darkest period of my life. I was angry with the world and angry at God. I didn't know what to do, but... Alcohol did!

The next five years would be a whirlwind of drunken nights. By the end, I was **BEYOND BROKEN**. I was ready to give up and be done with this world. I got to a point of drinking over forty beers a day. I had maxed out my funds and was in terrible standing with my job. My health was quickly deteriorating, and my anxieties and depression had me by the balls.

I suffered constant panic attacks and brain fogs. Not even knowing what day it was. Not showering or eating for days. I would wake up gasping for air. It was in the last months that I would hit my knees every night and pray in a drunken rage. *God!!! Make me a better father, friend, brother, and son... Save me from me!*

In reaching out to my ex-wife, in not knowing where to turn, but knowing I wasn't ready to die... I found myself at Mariposa Detox Center in Hollywood, CA. I took the leap of faith. For the first time in my life, I reached out for help. My life was unmanageable, and I was powerless to alcohol. It controlled my every move.

Alcohol's destruction progressed from my first drinks, to learning in high school it numbed reality so I could take on this world of weird energies. It went from drowning my problems away to drowning my existence on dry land. Twenty-four years later, Alcohol threw its last punch, and did it ever land hard.

Hope y'all are ready for life on life's terms, for it was in my weaknesses that I learned God is my strength. The next part of this book is my first two years in sobriety, and as a new creation in Christ. Time for redemption, restoration, and becoming a new man.

In the greatest humbling in my life, I realized I accepted Christ but never got to know him. I never gave thanks for anything in my life, and shortly after returning home, it all changed...

I recall waking up August 27th, 2022, and opening the Meeting Guide App on my phone. I had downloaded it the night before. The app showed every AA meeting in the area, based off your cell phone location. I saw there was a meeting at Adventure Church in Davenport, IA, at 10AM.

The meeting said it was closed and my heart started to race. I knew I needed this, but to walk this alone, I had to step out in faith. The group was called the Marquette Group.

I stumbled in, and I'm sure every ounce of my confusion showed. I mentioned that the app said the meeting was closed, and asked if I was in the wrong place. They asked if I had a desire to quit drinking, and I said that I definitely did. They motioned me to come in and take a seat, and told me I had arrived at the right place.

I had a great time listening to everyone share, and I was glad and thanked God for leading me to a great group so fast. I was then off to surprise my kids. Especially my daughter for her four-teenth birthday. She was under the impression I was staying in California for another two weeks or so. Even with the COVID crap, the school was cool with me coming in and surprising my daughter.

She instantly busted into tears when she saw me. I know I was crying, and pretty sure all the ladies at the front desk were teary-eyed, too. We embraced in a tight hug, and I didn't want to let her go. (If you are crying as the reader, just imagine me crying and trying to type a book.) My son rolled in with a big smile on his face, and I gave him a big hug. We left for lunch, and I spent the rest of the day with the kids.

One thing I needed to do with the kids was address the way their mother was on the runaround. I instantly nipped it in the bud. I didn't want to just come back and start laying down the law, but they were in need of structure, and quick. I was back and I wanted them to know that I wasn't messing around. It took a minute, but after a few arguments, we all seemed to be on the same page.

With AA, I quickly took on a sponsor. Not sure if I did the ninety meetings in ninety days, but I was hitting them twice a day, or whatever I could to establish a foundation fast. My sponsor was a cool older gentleman. I expressed to him I wanted to start step work as soon as possible, and really getting my hands dirty in my recovery. Just so happened, my home group AA at Adventure Church had a lot of long-term sobriety. A bunch of old timers, but I wouldn't have it any other way. I knew I would definitely need the mentorship.

Although Marquette Group was gold, I went into another group in Bettendorf, IA. This group was just starting up, and it was a faith-based 12-step program. It was here I met a cool old chap named Jack. He said he could see the fire in my soul. It was also here that I met Carlee.

The Bettendorf group was short-lived on my behalf, but in meeting Carlee I transitioned to Cornerstone Church in Eldridge, IA. It was here I tied into Life Recovery Group. This was another faith-based 12-step program. Carlee had launched the program at the church. She was around my age, and her passion to help people was right up my alley. She had a powerful testimony, and she was a beautiful person inside and out.

I was doing this thing. I was finally starting to feel proud of myself, for the first time in a long time. Although busy, I was eagerly awaiting returning to work, and I finally got the call. It was back to work and getting some income coming in. Phewwwww...

What a relief! I definitely got some strange looks, but said my hello's, and was off to a safety deal.

As I sat there doing my safety training on the computer, I told myself, "Ok Jeff, you ruffled a lot of feathers and broke a lot of relationships. Just lay low, my man, and get back to grinding…"

A few short hours later, I heard my name called over the intercom to come to the front office. *Ahhhhh, man. What now?* I was brought into a meeting with a bunch of head staff, HR, and my business rep for the union. I was fired on the spot, based on a story they had time to twist while I was away in rehab. It caught myself and the union rep completely off guard.

Although my gut dropped, I had a sense of peace. I knew that things would be all right. I didn't really care to work in factories, and in a sense, I would never leave during my addiction because it fed it. Now that I was sober, I was on to new beginnings. I prayed for strength to stay sober and for God to reveal himself in this situation.

I was ready to be done with that chapter of my life. But what to do with my time now? There wasn't a whole lot I could do, and the company agreed to pay unemployment as long as I didn't fight through union litigation. I took their bargaining agreement, and then, to my luck, they contested my unemployment. They withdrew from it, but since it was COVID Era, my unemployment payments didn't hit until December 7th, 2020.

My sponsor kept my spirits up, and got me hired with one of his friends, doing fencing. Although I was grateful to have work, I was only getting paid $12.00 an hour. It was solid work, though, and got me moving again until my unemployment kicked in.

Even though my job situation wasn't quite up to par, my relationship with the kids seemed to be getting better. That was, until my son thought driving illegally was a privilege he earned by getting a car to drive. I caught him dead in his tracks. I remember standing in his grandparents' living room. He was trying to act all tough in front of his friends. I stayed calm, but the kid was about thirty seconds from getting an ass-whooping none of those boys would forget. He ended up handing over the keys, which was in his best interest.

Around this time, I reached out to an old employer about construction work. I had built post frame for him before I went to work at the factory. To my luck, when I was in California, the Derecho storm had hit the Midwest. He told me he had all kinds of work, and I could start immediately.

This jump-in job would soon become a pivotal point in my life, in all sorts of ways. I went from barely scraping by to getting a decent nest egg saved up. Life seemed to be taking a turn for the better. One of my old bosses took me under his wing. Being close to thirty years sober himself, he completely supported my sobriety journey. I went from doing sliding door repairs to working for both of his subcontractors.

That December, life changed REAL QUICK. It was a beautiful day, about 50 degrees with the sun beaming down. I was working on a roof and kicking ass. Two old-timers and myself did purlins on our side faster than two crews on the opposite side. I was asked to tie in the first bay on the opposite once we finished.

I remember telling him no, and then I smiled at him. Instead of walking around the building, I decided to climb up the side we had already put roof on. As I went to pull myself up on the eave board… wissshhhttt!!! The nails released. I recall saying, "Oh, S**T!" but the guys said I didn't yell anything. They looked over when they heard a thud, but couldn't see me.

After about a twenty-five foot fall, I was air-lifted to University of Iowa Hospitals. I had broken my left arm at the elbow and the forearm bone had pushed through the skin. I had fractured my femoral head from impact on my hammer holder, along with multiple ribs. To top it off, I had a minor brain bleed and concussion… that brain injury I spoke of early on, that I was trying to remember.

I woke up to my mom sitting next to me in ICU. I asked her where I was. I was dazed! She told me I had fallen off a building and that I was lucky to be alive. I guess I scared the crap out of everyone in the family. Mom said that, regardless of the outcome, God had put on her heart that everything was going to be okay. Around 3 AM, my brain bleed stopped.

After seven long days in ICU, I was, more or less, kicked out of the university hospital for my parents to decide what to do with me. I hadn't seen any of my family, due to the COVID crap restrictions. My mother was the only one allowed to come visit me. I then found myself in a nursing home, kicking it with a bunch of eighty-year-old women.

Can't say I thanked God as much as I should have for being alive. Instead, I wondered why. "Why this, Lord!?!?" Things were going so well. I guess maybe too well, but as I sat there in a wheelchair, I couldn't help but be saddened. My whole life had changed in the blink of an eye, and now at age thirty-six, I sat wondering what life had in store for me. Would I be handicapped for the rest of my life?

Although, with a sense of disbelief, I tried to make the best of it. My parents made my nursing home apartment as homey as possible. I knew it wouldn't be my forever home, so I accepted what it was. About two, maybe three weeks out from the fall, the pain finally set in. I was informed that in traumatic events like this, the brain blanks the pain out until a later date. That if a person felt the pain at the time of the incident, it could put them in to shock.

This was no joke! I woke up around 3AM in my recliner. Everything was throbbing and my head was spinning. I instantly became nauseous. Due to being a recovering alcoholic, I steered clear of pain meds when I checked out of the hospital.

All I had was 500mg Tylenol. Let's just say I learned a whole next level of pain tolerance. I was praying to the Lord like no other. I acknowledged the pain and that Jesus had endured far worse before being crucified, but this guy was hurting.

The following weeks led me on an interesting journey. I tapped into my creative side to take my mind to a different space. I took to art. It had been a minute since I drew anything, but I had paper and pens and pencils. I started posting them to my Instagram and Facebook. In a short time, I tapped into my pre-existing skill, and my father's co-worker (a fellow artist) bought me a sketch pad and art supplies.

I had my mother grab my acoustic guitar as well. I wasn't even sure if I would be able to play it anymore, due to the arm breaks. Something I realized I had kind of taken for granted. I slowly formed chords and was instantly relieved. I even found my surgeon on Facebook and sent him a video of me playing.

During my time settling in to the nursing home, many people stopped in to help me out. It was nice to see old faces. My nonprofit business partner stopped in, my AA sponsor came through, and my old boss had been stopping by and bringing me snacks.

I found out the easiest way to get my parents to visit me was to nearly die, and then get moved down the road from them. Not to be taken in a bad way because I know life is ours to live and it gets busy, but it was definitely nice, being able to see them. Kind of odd, though, being thirty-six and having your mom help you shower, but I didn't have too many options at the time.

It was really nice reuniting with my brother. Not the way I would have planned it out, but what do they say? Man makes plans and God laughs. This really was sinking into my life. My brother and his wife took turns bringing me supper. It definitely beat the nursing home food. People pay all that money to be in one and then the food is atrocious.

My sister and her son also made frequent visits. I realized that I wasn't alone. I had just isolated from the world. There were people in my life that loved me, and would do whatever they could to help me in times of need. It was something that really sunk in, and put me in tears quite a few times.

It was also in this time that I came to terms with the child I had never met. There is a long story behind it, and I thought he was getting adopted. We lived separate lives. Out of the blue, his mother reached out to me, and we ended up meeting for the first time.

It was definitely awkward. Over ten years of never meeting and then there we stood, face to face. He was extremely shy the first time we met. Almost as if he had seen a ghost. Which for his entire life, I pretty much was. I took to playing some Xbox with him to try and find a level to relate. He had a lot of my characteristics, for damn sure.

I didn't really know how to take it all in, but in God's will for my life, I took this as one of the pieces of the puzzle. Not really sure where it would go, but the face-to-face meetup had taken place. I remember talking in California about it with Casey in Group. He reassured me that it would work itself out and be cool, and shared a story of a similar experience. He ended up being right.

Although art and music had taken off at this time, my son went off the rails. I'm more than sure he was scared, and his mom wasn't really in the picture, since she was hot after some new guy. Came to find out later, when he moved in with me that this was a time he was partying hard and skipping school almost every day.

One time, my son refused to come to my place for the weekend. I came to find out he had planned a huge party at his mom's house, because she had hopped a flight to Florida with her sister to see her newest fling.

I told him that if he wasn't there when I picked up my daughter that I would have the cops called on him, and that he better not be driving. I remember him telling me, "Good luck finding me!" He then quit responding to me. I told him, "I won't. I'm in a wheelchair. But the cops will."

I ended up putting him on the runaway list at the police station. His mom tried saying it wasn't a big deal, but there wasn't enough trust there, and she was nowhere in the picture right now. I could say that I was more than heated at this moment. Tough love in parenting... Ohhhhh, the joy!

That Sunday, I caught him at the local bowling alley. Just so happened when I told him not to drive that his car was parked right there in the parking lot. I once again called the police. I wanted to roll my happy ass up there in my wheelchair and grab him by the neck in front of his friends. But the cops insisted that I leave and promised they would handle things.

They went into the bowling alley and pulled him out in front of all his peers. They contacted his grandfather (his mom's side) and forced him to come get the car. It was in his name, and they had given it to my son on some verbal agreement. Not sure what all went down, but pretty sure it hit a nerve, because the kid didn't get behind the wheel again until he acquired his license.

My son later realized my tough love, and ended up thanking me for what I did. What he couldn't see I was doing at the time, ended up saving him from a life of no license. After seeing friends lose their licenses, he later understood he was on the verge of jeopardizing a freedom he didn't want taken from him. This tough love was very difficult. I explained to my son that it wasn't like I woke up in the morning and asked myself how I could ruin my son's day.

Before the fall, I would have operated completely different in self-will. In situations like this, I would have resorted to getting hammered, and then launched a verbal assault because I knew I couldn't be present. My son also knew at that time that I couldn't drive up and find his ass. He can later thank God, God had good intentions through all these trials.

At that time, my daughter sided with her brother. He was her ride everywhere, and he insisted that she wouldn't walk to school. That if she had to walk, that she wouldn't go. It was a challenge to provide structure, but I took accountability for my own actions in being caught up in my addiction, and that after my divorce, I gave the kids back to this woman, knowing that I couldn't trust myself in what I would do. I knew it was going to be tough, but that the structure was needed.

Amidst all this chaos, I thought I was doing fabulous things in my physical recovery. Trying to strengthen my arm with rubber bands and all that jazz. Come to find out, the doctors gave me terrible instructions on my arm. I was told to set the mobility brace from 0-60 degrees. My arm ended up healing at the elbow wrong.

They told me, Sorry for my luck, and I about jumped out the chair, bad hip and all. Around billing time, they started reaching out for me. I told them I was looking into lawyers due to my arm and then my physical care while at the hospital. Somehow, $200,000 in medical bills went to a balance of $0.00 in two days. I decided at that time I could deal with the gimp arm. Life on life's terms.

Through all this, I can honestly say that drinking was never on my mind. Not even a little bit. I had found ways to cope with the pain and struggles of parenting, and I knew deep down that I never again wanted to feel the way I had before leaving for California.

While in my art phase, I got into creating a TikTok profile. Something took me into just drawing people's pictures. Which led to drawing people who had passed away into a picture with the still living. I instantly grew a fan base, and I was humbled. I had told my daughter that the app was pointless and now, look at me go!

Once I got back up and moving, I was ready to go home. I secured a ride to get my truck, and I instantly felt the great pleasure of being able to come and go at my own convenience. Which also brought its own challenges. My head was still all messed up from the slam off the ground. Driving at night was almost impossible, and any weather change just about took me out.

I found driving from Eldridge to Muscatine for rehab to be quite the experience. My head would just start spinning and my vision would go blurry. Many times, I pulled over on the side of the road. At times, it would nearly put me to sleep. I would be driving, and my head would just drop as my eyes went closed.

I remember leaving the nursing home, saying goodbye to my lady friends, and looking around the room one last time. I went from wondering what I had done so wrong to deserve what had happened... to the idea that it was all starting to make sense. Whatever this season was in my life, I had pulled through it by God's good grace, and endeavored in areas of my life that I had previously given up.

Shortly after getting home, my old boss got me back doing some light duty work. It helped me get out of my headspace, and it was nice to get some fresh air. I was definitely hurting, but getting back to work felt good and brought some purpose back to my life.

That summer I was working for a subcontractor who was terrible. He started paying me one rate, then put me in charge of his crew and paid me less. He kept asking me if I just showed up whenever I wanted to. I was like... I'm not even supposed to be working until October. Yeah, I will do what I want... when I want!

Life was going good, and things were looking optimistic... and then the love bug came swooping in. A gal from my TikTok lives ended up living five miles away from me. Over a billion users on this platform and somehow, I connect in another person's live, in which I did a drawing for another artist.

Somehow we held off relationship status until my one-year sobriety, which I will touch on shortly. It was my first time dating sober, and, boy, was it a whole new world. Oh, I almost forgot a huge piece of the puzzle in my mental health.

In June, for Father's Day, my old construction foreman gave me a dog... RUFUS! He was a half black Lab, half Pointer. Pretty much a black Lab in a Pointer body. We instantly connected, and I ended up making him a service dog. It was nice coming home to him, and he poured love all over me. My dad asked why I got a dog. I said, "Well, it's kind of like coming home to Mom." He just laughed and shook his head.

This TikTok girl ended up inviting me to Passion Church at the mall in Davenport, Iowa. Kind of a weird place for a church, but it had an awesome vibe that instantly attracted me. They were a non-denominational church, and it reminded me a lot of the Tipton church where I had accepted Christ for the first time.

There was just something that seemed special about the place. It just so happened that the church was tied into a local faith-based addiction counseling center called 180. This also hit home. In trying to find as much sobriety community as I could, this piece of the puzzle fell right into place.

Right before my one-year sobriety in July of 2021, I commenced something that my heart had desired for quite some time. I got baptized on a Sunday with seventeen other people. It was the biggest group of baptisms the church had ever done. It was supposed to be done at a pond, which I was super excited about, but due to weather, we ended up in the church. Either way, this man got washed by the water, and what an amazing feeling.

Everyone showed up except my brother and his family. I know one is due to family circumstances and him removing himself from the circle, but the other is in his own identity in Christ and acknowledging God. I continue to pray for him and his family.

My mother, father, my sister and her son, my daughter, and even my grandma, all came to support my journey. Another key person that didn't show was my son. It kind of hurt, but ultimately, it was his decision, and I didn't show anger in his not attending.

Although we were good, he said that it was me getting baptized, not him, so why did he need to be there? He later told me he was being selfish and that he should have been there for me. He realized it was a big deal in my life and my sobriety, and that he should have been there to support me. I told him that all was good, and not to get down on himself. I smiled and said, "I mean, I could do it again, but it's kind of a one-time thing."

My one-year sobriety came on July 8th, 2021. I was a whirlwind of emotions. As I counted down the minutes and seconds, my eyes kept filling with tears, and I tried to hold myself together... Dang it!!! My eyes are all teared up just typing this up.

My daughter came down the night before to be with me, to celebrate it the next day at AA meeting.

My heart raced as the seconds slipped away towards 12:00 AM. When midnight struck, I bust out in tears, and pulled my daughter into a huge hug. I did it!!! One year of sobriety!!! Through everything, still standing and alive in God's good grace, and his mercy that never fails. He carried me when I couldn't carry myself, and now I stand free from the chains of addiction.

The next day my mom, daughter, and girlfriend all joined me to celebrate. My sponsor had gotten me an awesome 1-year chip. I stood before the group and spoke on how I did my first year. I had a sense of peace, love, and hope for my life moving forward. It was also nice hearing the people that came to support me share how they had seen me grow over the last year.

I put 100% into taking myself out of this world, so I put 100% into my recovery and creating its foundation. Addiction is self-centered, but to beat it, you must fight it with selfishness in your recovery. You have to be selfish in your recovery to become selfless in life. I pray each day to God for his strength and will for my life. For in my own will, I lead my life into destruction.

What seemed to be the longest year of my life actually flew right by. I was proud of myself for the first time in over 6-8 years. Heck, to tell the truth, I can't remember the last time before sobriety. I just always felt like a failure. All those months that I thought no one saw my transformation, and there they all sat, celebrating with me. I thanked God, first and foremost, for only in his will was it possible to be redeemed from the depths of hell that I had taken myself to.

So, in living "One Day at a Time," it was back to work. One day, my head contractor just about pulled over the building on the other workers as I was talking to my boss. Two guys were inside, and the building was an inch from collapsing. I looked at my boss and said I was done that moment. I ended up taking on a small project in Durant and two guys from his crew came with me.

In this time, I would lean on TikTok Live. I accumulated

followers and took to painting random pictures. After work, I would be in pain, and getting on the live and painting took my mind away from it. It was an app that I had hassled my daughter about, and now I was making money off it. It also gave me a chance to start sharing my testimony. It was odd because my mom had gotten me paints for Christmas, and I was like... I don't paint. She said, "Well, I think that maybe you will."

One night at, like, three in the morning, a guy sent me $200 on Venmo after I had shared my story. I had still been going to the Life Group in Eldridge and I donated the money to the group to get recovery Bibles. I guess you could call it one of those "AHA!" moments. Be open and transparent about how God has been, and still is working in my life and, "Boom!"

August came rolling in and it was a pivotal month. I took a leap of faith and started up my own business. Rise Up Construction, LLC was born at the end of August. Right as that great news came through, I had planned a trip for my daughter's fifteenth birthday to go to the Rocky Mountains.

The girlfriend's sister lived out there so I figured we would make a trip out of it so we could see the mountains, and she could visit her sister that she spoke of missing so much. Through Airbnb, I was able to rent an awesome little house at a town near Denver. We chose to road trip... not tooooo bad of a drive, but Matte almost ran us out of gas before we even got out of Iowa.

The Rockies trip is one I will never forget. First and foremost, it was the first vacation I had taken with my kids when I was sober. Past vacations had always consisted of winding down the nights getting hammered, like I deserved a reward for taking these heathens on a trip. The typical excuses of an alcoholic, looking for a reason to suck down some poison.

The next awesome thing was the overwhelming greatness of God's creation. Those mountains are something else. The weather was beautiful, and the views were amazing. Just recognizing how small we are in comparison to this beautiful world. It was hands down the coolest thing I have ever witnessed with my naked eye.

While out there, we also checked out the graffiti in downtown Denver. Talk about some cool paintings. We got a lot of pictures. Another cool place that I will be back to visit for a Christian concert is Red Rocks Amphitheatre. Has to be about the coolest outdoor venue known to man. We got to watch people exercise up and down the seating, but no music. I could only imagine the sounds that place would put off.

While my daughter went shopping with the girlfriend for her birthday, my son and I had some father/son bonding time. I signed for him to get his first tattoo. I took pictures during the whole thing. The tattoo artist ended up screwing up, but pulled off an even cooler tattoo. Went from a two-hour piece to a four-hour piece for the same price.

One downfall to the trip was the start to the end of the relationship with the girlfriend. I had ignored quite a few red flags, but in meeting her sister all kinds of crazy came lurking out. It seemed like there was some kind of suppressed trauma from the past, and some kind of resentment towards her sister.

The good thing I thought I was doing in going to see her sister, because she supposedly missed her... well, let's just say it just went to pieces in a hurry. A huge victim role came on, and she instantly turned the trip into something she didn't feel she was supposed to be on. That we were just doing our thing, and she wasn't a part of the family. All three of us were more than taken back.

The last night of the trip ended up with her throwing a fit and me sleeping on the floor by my son. The drive home was odd, and when we got back to Iowa, I called her out. I told her I didn't know what she had going on, but I wasn't about to play the games.

A few days after, we went out for ice cream, and talk turned to her ex. Which she said we had agreed to not talk about. I was like, okay. Next thing, she was screaming and yelling and just about swung on me, then told me to get out of her car. It was like a four-teen-year-old girl throwing a tantrum. I smiled and said, "You don't have to ask me twice." I told her to figure out what she wanted, and if it wasn't me, to bring my stuff back. I came home

the next day to find my stuff sitting outside the door of my apartment, and just like that, it was over.

This ended up being a true test of faith for me. To date, it was
the closest that I have come to relapse. It is no joke when the
counseling groups say no dating in the first year. All my other
break-ups, I turned straight to alcohol. This time hit different.
Despite all my accomplishments and moments that made me
proud, I sunk into a depression fast.

This was the first time I actually sat and processed emotions. I
remember I slept all Saturday and skipped church that Sunday. I
thought, why do I even try? Why did I open up my heart? I will
never find love... I prayed hard and had my pity party for one.
And then it hit me. What would bringing out the old me do to fix
anything? I also recognized that it's okay to have feelings and be
sad. I didn't have to numb my life.

One thing that hit a nerve was a sense of being judged, and
letting it get to me. One of her friends from church had said that I
wasn't a "godly man," and that I was no good for her. Maybe this
was what lit my fire, but I was just an infant to this born-again
Christian thing.

I ended up going all in on God. She ended up leaving the
church after three weeks of crying on everyone's shoulder, while I
sat alone and felt like I was cast out as a terrible person. I started
going to Bible studies on Saturday morning, and got in a leadership team at the church. All in all, I can't speak too bad of her. She
has some of her past to cope with, but she led me to Passion
Church.

I kind of wondered, okay, God, you got me to this church, and
I see where I fit in, but why the test with the heart? I guess it is just
part of the story, and that in turning to him instead of alcohol, my
life stayed its course for the good. All I know is that in God's will
for my life, sometimes the plans get messy because I'm not in
control. Which I am learning to be okay with.

In this time, I got to know a younger lad named Kris, and my
soon-to-be God mom, LeeAnn. Kris was in the 180 program. He

had some trials in life, but he was a hard worker who seemed to have a good head on his shoulders. He ended up helping me at work when I struggled to find help. On our drives to work, I opened up to him about my relationship with the ex-girlfriend and life in general.

So, on top of the break-up, firing almost my entire crew, and the physical pain of a six-inch screw backing out of my leg (I came to find out the blood supply didn't take on my femoral head and the screw started backing out), I was on some next level praying. LeeAnn ended up being a godsend. She didn't even want to do the leadership team, but had said God moved her to do so, and she was obedient.

One day in class, I was in extreme pain. LeeAnn went in to pray for me after class. As she prayed with her hand on my shoulder... her eyes got big, and she lit up. She looked me in the eyes and said, "Did you know you have an anointing over your life?"

I just looked at her, discombobulated in the fact I didn't have the faintest clue what she was talking about. She briefly explained what my anointing was, and you could say that I was kind of awestruck. I didn't really know what to say. My mom told me before I left on my flight to California that she saw me one day traveling the U.S. telling my story. Now standing before me, a woman I had never met, shared that I had an anointing over my life to do just that. WOW!

That Sunday at church, she gifted me this little black book that said "Faith," and inside of it was a folded up paper that had my anointing written out on it:

Jeff – received Feb. 10ᵗʰ, 2022, from LeeAnn
Genesis 32:22-32

Book ministry and youth outreach
"Broken Pieces" Redeemed, Restored, Renewed
Jacob wrestles with God till he is blessed
Jacob becomes "Israel" – one must first submit to God to be blessed.

1. *Jacob was missing the affirmation of his father, so God left a physical reminder of his "weakness"*
2. *Jacob was a hustler, then one day he was alone with God. (Relentless to struggle with God) God became his God during the wrestling match.*

You can't rely on "your own" strength, so perseverance was rewarded, now Jacob is "Changed." He has a "new name." Living his "new identity." He had to "lose to win," and so in his weakness he is now strong through Christ.

2 Corinthians 12:10 God's power is your weakness. God is our Source. He allowed our weakness to occur in order to draw us to Him – so that we look only to Him to receive strength!

I started out the book she gave me with writing a blank check to Jesus Christ for the redemption of my life. I had heard someone talk on this and instantly felt conviction to write out this blank check for my life. Because from here on out, I would surrender my will to his and do what I could to serve others for him.

Two days after getting this anointing letter from LeeAnn, I found myself at an AA meeting. It was there that my sponsor, Don, asked if I would host an AA meeting at the Scott County Jail. All I could think was, Dang! This is God's will for my life and my anointing stuff sure works fast.

It was around this time that I went to a Wednesday night service, after which I jumped on Scott, our praise leader, about playing guitar for him. He said sure and asked me to play some chords for him. I didn't get past playing three lines, and he stopped me and asked for my email.

I was thinking to myself that this was awesome. In the near future, I would get a chance to play with the praise band. The next day, I got an email to play that Sunday. Oh, s**t! I haven't been playing in front of a crowd in seventeen years and now I'm doing it in three days.

This ended up being a huge blessing in my life. I was able to get back to pursuing passions that I had put by the wayside. That first Sunday, though… talk about nervous as all get out. I had a stern look on my face the entire time, and my eyes never left the iPad that had the music on it. To this day, I still get some nerves right before we start, but I wouldn't trade it for the world. I love being up there praising the Lord with my music abilities.

Over the winter, my leg really started to put the hurt on me. I thought I had pulled my pelvis, but I came to find out it was way worse. Like I mentioned earlier, the screw they had put in was backing out of my femur. My chiropractor did X-rays, and we saw it had backed out almost a half inch. The blood supply never took. So, the bone healed, but the area above the break died. It was disintegrating inside me and the screw had nothing to hold onto.

I was physically pushing myself to the limits, all the while on no pain medication whatsoever. My pain tolerance was in extreme mode. For about three months, I would come home, and the muscles would freeze up. It would take me a good thirty minutes just to limp myself into my apartment. Somehow I pushed through ten-hour work days in the dead of winter.

One day, I was doing an interior liner package for a guy, and nothing that day was going right. I was losing my temper and slammed the steel sheet up against the wall. In doing so, I deeply lacerated my left palm and started bleeding out profusely. My co-worker luckily had a janky first aid kit that had some butterfly Band-Aids.

He taped it up the best he could, and it was back to work. There was blood all over my clothes and the floor… Such a nice look! Then my phone rang. What now? It was the University of Iowa. After viewing my X-rays, they decided I had to have a full hip replacement. GREATTTTT… Back under the knife and more time off work, while already struggling to keep the business going.

I recall looking up and saying, "Lord, I don't know what's going on, but it is as if someone died or something." And then my phone rang again. This time it was my mother, and she started out the conversation with, "Well, I hate to tell you this way... but your father has stage 4 lung cancer that has spread to the brain." Welllll, f**k me! The world seemed to stop for a second and my heart dropped. I wasn't quite sure how to process this information.

On the drive home from work that night, I had a moment of God's love so vast I cannot explain it. I was headed south on Highway 61 and the sky was something else. A beautiful sunset to my right, dark blues to the left, and pitch black with lightning bolts striking directly in front of me to the south.

This was so metaphorical of my life at the moment. Just like my drive home, I was headed directly into a big storm. Although it was a very stressful situation, I was at complete peace. A peace I couldn't even comprehend. A surreal calm overtook me, and I knew at that moment that everything would be okay. The battle belonged to him, and he reassured me of that. In God's will, I was at complete peace, going head on into this raging storm.

I won't lie... I was pushing myself to the max, physically and mentally, but amidst the storm I continued to hit AA meetings, Bible studies, and my leadership group. Heck, I could barely get up on the stage, but I took every chance offered to me to get up there and praise the Lord. I wasn't minding the physical pain so much anymore, and I knew I would go to any length to avoid feeling the way I felt before boarding that plane to California.

Although I had staffing issues and battles with my hip, business was starting to take shape. Although facing many many hurdles, the crew got better with each job. Some days I wondered how I even kept pressing on, but I put my faith in Jesus. I knew that the pain and suffering I faced were nothing compared to what he went through, in being crucified to cleanse humanity of our wrongdoings.

Up through March, I somehow found time to paint. It was my winter gig. I ended up pulling off an awesome collage painting of Jesus. I gifted the painting to different people that were instrumental in the foundation of my faith, and the original went to

Brandy off TikTok. She had been a regular in my TikTok lives and had asked if I would paint her something.

End of March was a night I will never forget. I had asked my mom to buy tickets to Zach William in Cedar Rapids, IA. I ended up taking Kris with me, the dude from 180 that helped me at work, to show my gratitude for him stepping in and creating a friendship. Hands down, the best concert I've ever been to in my life, and I was sober. I ended up seeing an old co-worker and got to catch up. Man was the Holy Spirit ever moving in that place.

Speaking of that night… On the drive home I missed our exit, and somehow got navigated by the place I was going for my hip replacement. I didn't know it at the time, but it was as if God was showing me where I would be next, and that he was in control of the situation.

God has done this to me multiple times now. Something out of the ordinary happens, and I later come into the people or places where I was meant to be.

At the end of our leadership group at Passion Church, we were given the assignment to do a sermon in front of the group. I missed the class when they announced it and I remember being lost in the next group meeting. After a half hour of trying to make sense of all the information I was getting, I stopped Nathan, our associate pastor, and he informed me we were doing a 5-10 minute sermon. Ohhhhhhh, now it makes sense.

I recall sitting with Leeann, and almost in panic asking questions. I haven't read the Bible… I don't know what verse to go to… How will I ever pull this off?

Ideas started flooding my head as Luann spoke words over me from the Bible that related to my life. I kind of started wondering if my life was taking me to a place that I would preach. This next piece is what I came up with for the sermon:

FINDING A NEW IDENTITY IN CHRIST
Surrendering our will to God's will,
In that we become a new creation

Mathew 10:39

Whoever finds life will lose it, and whoever loses his life for my sake will find it.

Such a powerful verse we have here. I actually have it on my flesh, and at the time I had it tattooed, it didn't make sense to me. Today in my newfound spiritual journey, surrendering my will to God's will for my life has come to make complete sense.

Let us bow our heads:

Lord, thank you for bringing us together tonight to rejoice in your Word. For people new to preaching your Word, we ask that you guide the words to bring you honor, Lord. May our hearts and ears remain open to receive the messages that are shared tonight, that we may each take something from these sermons to help us move forward in blind faith in our walks as Christians.

The big question, "Have we fully surrendered our lives to walk with Christ?"

We each have a heart of fear, to say the least. Can I relinquish control of my life to an unseen God in blind faith, in hopes that my life will be one of peace and eternal life? I have heard people speak of this truth, but is it actually for me as well? I mean, I accepted Jesus… doesn't that mean I'm good?

Matthew 16:24-26

24 Then Jesus told his disciples, "If anyone would come after me, let them deny themselves and take up their cross and follow me. 25 For whoever would save their life will lose it, but whoever loses theirs for my sake will find it. 26 For what will it profit a person if they gain the whole world and forfeit their soul?

Here we see these same words again. That if we live a life in our own will, we will lose it, but if we live a life for Christ, we find life. In my mid-twenties, I was attending a little church in Tipton, IA. My construction foreman knew I was going through a hard time with my kids as a single dad, and he told me I should try out the church. It was at this church that I had my first memorable encounter with the Holy Spirit. As the church body sat with their heads down in prayer, something that felt like a fire encompassed my body and an unknown power lifted my hand to accept Christ as my savior.

I remember clenching my fist and punching him in the leg. "WHAT JUST HAPPENED?!?!" I asked. With a smile on his face, he said, "You felt the Holy Spirit, didn't you?" And he just kept on grinning. So, I started in this new life, but it was a life I didn't understand. In just a few short years, I met my wife, got my kids back in my life, became a volunteer firefighter, started a nonprofit... I was on top of the world. All that I touched turned to gold. ME! ME! ME! I gave no thanks to the God who orchestrated it., Instead, I kept saying, thank you, Jeffrey, for being so awesome. (Can anyone relate? Thinking everything is going well because you are awesome?)

At that time, I didn't get to know Christ and walk as a Christian. I didn't pick up my cross and walk in his will. I soon found out it can all disappear, just as fast as it was gifted. I lost a two-year court battle for primary custody of my kids, ended up in divorce, and went from looking at $300k homes to a one-bedroom apartment. So, what does one do? Well, I blamed God, and so started my battle. Alcohol consumed me. Instead of turning to God, I turned my back and tried to drown my reality. I took myself to the darkest of places.

Which brings me to the parable of the Prodigal son. This is where I became the one that Jesus left the ninety-nine for. God was more than patient with me as I drove myself to the depths of Hell, ruining every aspect of my life.

*If we can look **at Luke 15:11-32**, where Jesus spoke of a man who had two sons. Where the younger son asks for property, then he runs off and wastes his newfound wealth in frivolous living, bringing his family to ruins. In his own will, he destroys his life, then looks at his brother and father and the servants' lives in jealousy. "But why is it* *they have it better than me?" he wonders. In this moment, the younger brother humbles himself and comes to Christ.*

This was me on my journey. Not sure if any of you can relate, but when we set off in our own will, we find ourselves in complete turmoil, with everything that was given by the father no longer intact. We find ourselves wrestling with God.

Here I come to Jacob and his wrestle with God.

I always had this notion of being a leader and having this calling. God's timing is perfect, and he takes his time to refine us. Never in a million years would I have thought to go through what I went through to get where I am at today. To break generational curses and be chosen in my family line to be "that one." God knows exactly what he is doing.

It was in my wrestle with God to maintain control that I had the answers; that in losing control, I found my life. My addiction had defeated me, and I can only be forever grateful that I reached a point of desperation, that in my wrestling with God I had no choice but to fully surrender my will. My will alone wouldn't bring a life of peace and purpose.

Since the day of turning my will over to God's will and picking up my cross, my life has been found in many ways. I'm approaching two years sober. I have started my own company. My daughter has accepted Christ and was baptized. My son has moved in with me. I now have Jesus riding co-pilot and I give thanks every day. I am active in my church and the recovery community, and back on stage playing guitar. The old me is no longer. In Christ, I am a new being. I also have a group of people that keep me moving forward in my new life in Christ and I know that it's okay to ask for help.

Genesis 32:28

> *Then he said, "Your name shall no longer be called Jacob, but Israel, for you have striven with God and with men and have prevailed.*

Through much time and wrestling with God, I realized that God never left me. Instead, I left God on my own will, to prove to the world I could do it all by myself. I chased pleasures of the flesh, temptations, and desires, and got to a point so low and so empty. I reached out my hands and there was my Savior, awaiting my return.

In conclusion, not one of us asks to be here. One day, we come into this world. We don't get to pick our parents or home life. Then one day, we reach an age where we cast ourselves among a body of sinners in a sea of temptation and desires, trying to find peace and purpose. In our own will, we tend to get lost in this vast world, and we hold on so tightly to what little control we think we have.

Have you let go? Have you surrendered your will? Not just accepted Christ, but have you picked up your cross and walked in his will.? God is patient and your new identity awaits you, as in the verse,

Matthew 10:39

Whoever finds his life will lose it, and whoever loses his life for my sake will find it.

I got overly busy with the weather getting nice, but I managed to get the Jesus painting to its home on May 6th, 2022. Between my femur deteriorating and no surgery till June 1st, it was taking all and everything of me to keep moving. Work, AA, church, construction projects… I was bound and determined to wear that sucker out before I got a new one.

To add to projects completed, I got the welcome center up and going for the church. It was like a fancy bar style counter that was L-shaped. To think I quit drinking and built my best bar to date. Not that I would be one to have ten projects going at once, but I slowly was getting some completed.

One thing that I had noticed was my ability to feel energies. I guess it is called discernment, but I like to call it being empathic. I had never realized that I got drawn to alcohol quickly in my teen years and early twenties because I absorbed other's anxieties. For some reason, I thought it was a good idea to numb those absorbed feelings by destroying myself with alcohol. Nowadays, I do a lot of observing and praying instead of absorbing and self-destructing.

I noticed that a lot of times when I was up on stage, I would get overwhelmed. A few songs into playing in the praise band, and I would go haywire. My vision went blurry, and the sound got muffled, and I also felt a pounding sensation.

When new 180 members came into church and their hearts were opening to the Holy Spirit, it was as if I could sense their spiritual attack or something. God must have taken over, because I would just keep strumming until I got a chance to pray. This was quite new to me, and it was rocking me pretty good. I leaned on talking to LeeAnn to try and understand exactly what was happening.

This brought so much understanding as to why I became best friends with alcohol so early. I took on a bunch of anxiety in high school, and I was always a nervous wreck. Alcohol calmed the storm and made me feel like I was normal. I just needed me some Jesus, but this prodigal son took off in self-will.

With alcohol, I was ten feet tall and bulletproof. There wasn't anything I feared... I thought. To realize in the end that I operated in complete fear, with zero ability to manage my own life. The best friend that numbed reality did everything in its power to put me in my grave and leave me empty, with anxieties raging.

June came quick and before you know it, I had a new hip. I was pretty much at ease going into surgery. Dave, my business seller, took lead on my crew and had them build some small projects. I had my finances in check, and a great support system. Surgery went awesome and I was back to work in ten days. I was starting to wonder if I could use a couple more new hips in different places of the body.

With the new hip and pain to the wayside, I was more than optimistic about Summer and getting back to work. The business was thriving, and life was good. I recognized that when hard times came up in my life, I found myself in prayer. That and I was looking for guidance in my community to come up with solutions, instead of playing victim. I could definitely sense myself losing my edge, and I was trying to trust the process more and more.

July 8th, 2022, came and it was a flood of tears, complemented with a huge smile. TWO YEARS SOBER! No alcohol or nicotine. This was the excerpt from my Facebook post that morning.

Some days, it seemed like the odds were stacked against me. From falling off a building, to finding out my dad had stage 4 cancer, to having to go back under the knife for a total hip replacement. Struggles of starting my own business and raising my teenage son as a single father because he made the decision to live with me full-time... some days have seemed never-ending, where others just went by way too fast, but today I'm just going to rest in this moment.

I have a long way to go, but I'm beyond proud of myself, especially in this world we live in today. To be two years sober of alcohol and nicotine is a huge accomplishment. Anxiety and depression have more or less gone by the wayside, and I have come to terms with a lot that I have been through.

In my infant stages of my newfound spirituality, I am learning a peace that won't be shaken. Glory be to God in the redemption of this prodigal son. Once drowning and trying to just survive... to living my life and learning to love myself again.

Taken from someone else, "I can now do and have all the things I once dreamed about while drunk." From getting baptized, getting back into art, playing guitar on stage for the praise band, going on a year operating my own construction company, to being financially stable, writing a book (this book), serving in the community, doing church projects and leadership groups, and being active in the recovery community... just to name a few. I can only say that I am more than optimistic about this next year and what is to come. A big thank you to all who have, and continue to support my journey.

The day was special. My mom came up for my AA meeting to see me get my 2-year chip. I told my testimony, and I got a total rash of crap for talking too much. Went from not being one to do public speaking, to being told, "Hey Jeff, wrap it up, Bud. There are more people in the room that want to share." I got that Holy Spirit activated and it doesn't like to be quiet. This is also a point where the fruits of my labors really started showing up.

An Xbox buddy from Texas that I had friended on Facebook saw that I didn't have a company logo. He ended up designing me an awesome logo for my business and surprised me with it. The second week of July, I had my first batch of T-shirts screen printed, and the following week I had hats embroidered.

I didn't think that the merch line would be a hit to my fellow Facebook community, but I ended up getting hit from all sides with people asking for hats and T-shirts. I guess this is what branding myself looks like. The Rise Up in my construction name actually came from the ex-girlfriend. She said, "Why don't you call it 'Rise Up?' You seem to rise up and conquer anything you set your mind to."

Just so happened that the original place in California I was supposed to go for recovery was also called Rise Up. This ended up fitting quite well, and it was how I ran my sobriety. No excuses! Rise up and go to any length to reach your goals.

Speaking of Xbox, there was another younger lad I played with named Jacob. I had also friended him on Facebook. One night, I got the chance to play with him, and I found out he had gotten sober and turned his life around. He said he followed my journey on Facebook, and that I inspired him to change for the better.

I screenshot the text and send it to Big Mike from Texas. Mike was of faith and had been through his own struggles. He was an open ear for me before I made the leap. Now this is what life is about. Some guys getting online to get away from the stresses of life, and not even knowing they became each other's support network.

Although my life had become super busy, I had also become

selfless. I had never made excuses to drink seven days a week, so I ran my sobriety the same. As long as I was serving others, I knew that I would be better than I was the day before. Something I preach in recovery is that you have to be selfish in your recovery to become selfless in life.

If we resort to our old ways and try to operate in self-will and relapse, then we will be right back to hell on earth. We will become self-centered and become the center of our broken universe. It's strange, but you have to fight the self-centered disease with selfishness. Without our sobriety and connection to God, we find ourselves right back in the devil's playground.

On July 29th, I dove headfirst into my first speaking engagement. I gave my testimony at a local AA meeting. I had prayed all week on how to start it off, and it finally came to me. A story of when I was camping with my parents. (Not to put any blame on them for my addiction.) I got to try my first wine cooler, and the cravings were there. Whatever it was, I wanted more. From the first time consuming alcohol, it had control of me.

The speaking engagement went very well, and my spiritual mentor, LeeAnn, showed up and I didn't even realize it. At the end of the testimony, I had to draw a card. One card specifically stood out to me. It almost appeared to be glowing. The card I grabbed was the chair LeeAnn was sitting in, and she didn't even know there where cards taped to the chairs. Coincidence??? I think not!

I originally hadn't planned on writing past my first two years in sobriety, but all I can say is things really started coming to life after that second year. One cool thing was going to Small Group at the pastor's house. I got accepted into his two sons' band they were starting because I could play guitar. In a matter of ten minutes, we wrote our first song from scratch. A seven-year-old drummer, a nine-year-old singer, and a 38-year-old kid on acoustic guitar.

We ended up performing the song live for everyone after dinner, and it was an instant hit. Glory be to God and the talent of these young children. An awesome experience that brought one of my passions back to life. I'm interested to see where the Lord takes this one. We planned to get 4-5 songs figured out so that we could take over the stage for Sunday service.

September rolled around and I embarked on another speaking engagement at the Scott County Jail. (Not in handcuffs this time... nice change of pace.) Our Marquette AA group was hosting AA meetings there for the inmates. I had been told, "Why would you do that? You're crazy!" My answer is quite simple. When we come to the light and become the salt of life, we can't season other people's lives if we leave the salt in the shaker.

The speaking went awesome, and I could really sense the Holy Spirit working through me. That first meeting, I had this vision of shaking all the inmates' hands. Which I guess is supposed to be a no-no in meetings. I wanted the inmates to know I respected them and that I was no better than any of them.

I instantly made connections with the majority of the group, and at the end of the meeting the inmates all came up and shook our hands. Which I think was unseen and unheard of. I could feel the fire (Holy Spirit) just rolling inside of me. Connecting with these men and making strides towards their breakthrough made me excited for the opportunity to speak more regularly.

September 10th was the next date that stood out to me as a monumental point in my journey. I was asked by our praise leader to play live for a fundraiser walk for a great group called Pregnancy Resources. They assisted in giving ultrasounds to less fortunate mothers in the attempt to reduce the number of abortions.

This was the first time playing live in public (gig style) in about twenty years. We played without a click track and we just went off the fly. I was having the time of my life in a beautiful location on the Mississippi riverfront. During one of our intermissions, the pastor's kids asked if we could perform our song. Not even a week after writing it, there we were.

Never in a million years could I have written this up. Breaking free of addiction, almost falling to my death, playing in a praise band, to playing a song that myself and a seven- and nine-year-old had written. Only God can orchestrate these kinds of stories. I was in absolute joy as we came to the end of the song and praising our Lord.

September was a big month. On the 15th, I had been playing some open tuning chord progressions. I had been dabbling for over a year with the chords. I wondered how I would ever come up with words. I came across a video on TikTok, and it gave me chords in the open tuning structure.

Right around midnight, sitting in my room, I came up with the words. In just over five minutes, I wrote the song, "I Need a Savior." I kind of surprised myself on this one, and even was able to sing it without sounding like a crying stray cat. God is good, all day, every day... even at 11:59:59PM.

September 18th, my nonprofit partner, Dan, had a fundraiser Euchre tournament for his birthday. We raised close to $1,000 to help local families undergoing unexpected hardships. This was something I had prayed about. Was this journey over? Was it time to throw in the towel? God, can you reveal yourself in this situation? The Holy Spirit was saying, "Don't give up just yet, my son!"

I'm not sure of the exact date, but I remember Dan coming to church. After service, we talked about life, and he had me in tears. He told me that he knew where I had come from, and how far I had come. That whatever I had in my life, he wanted, and that I was inspiring him to be a better human. That salt was seasoning, my cup was overflowing, and I was so grateful of God's presence and grace over my life.

There were a lot of awesome things going on. And not that I don't want to write a 1000-page novel, but I want to wrap this thing up before 2023 (as I sit here typing on January 28th, 2023, but we will get to that later.)

On October 29th, I finished the gambrel style barn the crew was building. With right around three years building experience and never owning a business, we pulled it off. It looked amazing and my seller had professional pictures taken of it. It was awesome doing a job I love, and being able to see the fruits of my labor.

That factory life was a drag. The blood, sweat, and tears were paying off.

The next day, on the 30th, the band was back at it. Josiah, the nine-year-old, had written another song. I gave it some structure, and in about fifteen minutes, the song, "Praise You," was born. That kid has a phenomenal voice, and a pure talent for singing and songwriting.

November 11th rolled around, and the church had an appreciation dinner for the volunteers, which they called the Dream Team. Hands down, I received one of the best awards I have ever been given. The prior year they gave out an MVP award, and I thought to myself, "How cool is that!" I decided to go all in this year to serve the Lord and the church selflessly.

For praise band, construction projects, Bible studies, and life groups, the pastor awarded me with the Passion Dream Team: Blood, Sweat, and Tears Award. Just over two years ago, I was ready to give up on life. I spent most all my time wasted with a hate for the world, and anger at God and myself.

In getting sober, accepting Christ, getting baptized, and getting out of my own way, I realized I barely waste time now. Each night, I lay my head to rest in peace, knowing I am advancing God's kingdom. Some days, I wake up wondering if this is still all a dream. Did this all really happen? Is this stuff right now actually happening?

A huge thank you to the pastor and praise leader for welcoming me, not only into their church, but also into their homes. This last year has been a testimony of blood, sweat, and tears, and I couldn't be any prouder of how far I have come, and how much I was able to help serve the church and its body. From early morning band practices, to closing down shop at midnight on a new drum booth... I wouldn't trade it for the world.

God is good, and I was honored to be able to serve in this capacity. Before, I had put my all into ending my life here on earth. But in Christ, I planned to put my all into serving his kingdom and living out his will for my life. Scott was always saying to build an altar, and I did just that. I took ownership not only in my life, but also in the place where I honored the Lord for redeeming my life.

Thanksgiving came around, and in ending the weekend, I saw vulnerability in the men in my life who had inspired me to become a better man, father, and son. In reaching the gift of desperation just two short years ago, I did a 180 and God turned my life around. In blind faith, I turned my will over to God's in hopes of a better life, and have I ever been blessed.

Something told me that day that I would lead prayer at my parents' house. Just so happened, we all took hands, and my mother looked at me and said, "Jeff, you can lead prayer this year." Just revisiting this has me all teary-eyed. My life has been nothing short of a miracle, but as long as God's in it the story isn't finished.

I know many people prayed for me over the years. Our praise leader led the service that morning, which was on encouraging and praying for others who lifted us up when we were down. I can't thank those people enough, not in just the last two years, but in all 38, for showing me God's grace and carrying me through when I couldn't carry myself.

Coming into December, we found out that Dad's cancer was attacking. The tumors had shrunk, but were back to growing. This news sucked, but Dad returned to work and went back to his old lifestyle of drinking and smoking. It's possible that the damage was already done, and Dad was just accepting fate. He kept saying he was going to die, anyway.

At one time, I questioned, why fight to live to chase an addiction? By God's grace, I have been pulled from addiction. But I guess, in his shoes, what would one do? Knowing you haven't accomplished everything you wanted in life and staring death in the face?

Since our family was still broken and couldn't come together, I thought the energy should have been focused at restoring the family instead of another round of chemo. I figured, you do you

Pops, and bow out gracefully. It was going to be a struggle either way. Just a crap scenario altogether.

This time, it hit my brother hard. Life was at stake and no healing had been made. All those times of burying the pain and living in denial, accepting what seemed to be the answer to the issue was coming to the surface and fast. It felt like I was being attacked from all angles "What do I do, Jeff?" "How do we do this, Jeff?" "What's next, Jeff?"

I turned to my prayer team and church family, but this time my prayers weren't in healing the cancer in Dad, but the cancer that destroyed our family. I asked them for prayers of family restoration. I hit my knees and gave it to God. I had talked with both sides, telling them that if pride and egos could be set aside, there would be room for healing. Through accountability of individual actions and forgiveness, that God could and would move mountains.

My brother went out, and they talked with my parents. Not real sure what all went down, but some kind of peace was made. For the first time in, like, seven years, my brother and his family were joining our parents for Christmas. My sister still wasn't in, but I guess we needed to take baby steps. God was beginning to move in the family, and I thanked him graciously.

December 19th, my dad was laid up in the ER with pneumonia and had developed sepsis. The doctors said he was lucky he hadn't started the chemo, because it would have taken his life. I remember going and sitting with my dad. He was very uncomfortable with any of us kids seeing him suffer. He mentioned that he had a lot of time to think in the hospital alone at night.

Dad came out of the hospital and gave quitting the bad habits a shot. I give full credit to him for showing his efforts to quit. Part of me felt that he had pictured his last days being spent hooked up to machines in a hospital room, with his loved ones watching him suffer. I think he had started to accept where this was leading.

This brings me back to the phone call with my parents when I was in rehab, and that it sucked coming back home to a broken family. Steph, the counselor, said, "Maybe God is using you in the family to show people can change and break generational curses."

Some days, we wonder why we go through all the struggles we do. Although some of our own hell is brought on by ourselves, we are soon humbled. God doesn't give us what we can't handle without him, and he goes into battle before us.

That day, after the call, I sat wondering, "Why me, Lord?" Living my life surrendered to Christ and doing his will, I am now seeing his plan for my life. In overcoming these generational curses and beating addiction, I had become the light in a family that was going through dark times. I had been taken through all this family destruction and hell, and through Christ I had found salvation, hope, and freedom. I am forever grateful.

This is where I wanted to wrap things up, but they say as long God's in it, the story isn't finished. On January 20th, 2023, just shortly after 11PM... Hold up. Can't type and cry... God stepped in and brought my father home. His battle was through and there was no more pain and suffering.

My parents had gone south on vacation to visit my mom's mother in Mission, TX. From what I knew, Dad had just gotten chemo, but seemed to be all right. Mom said he was on the move the entire time, and fiddling around, doing his thing, as usual. I remember sending a pic of the horse barn I was building and saying, "Hey, Dad! Remember when you said I would never do construction? Well, look at me now!"

Damn, is this difficult, typing this the same day we laid him to eternal rest... I was at work and received a text from my mother, saying Dad had pneumonia again, but that it should just be a little bump in the road, and he would be back to good soon. Something made me look over my shoulder and I saw my seller was sitting out front.

I went out to talk to him and birds swarmed the trees at the residence we were building. The noise they made was grand. We could barely converse. I remember saying, "God must be trying to tell us something. I returned to work and checked my phone.

There was a text from my phone saying to get the prayer warriors going because they couldn't get dad stabilized.

A million thoughts could have been racing, but once again in my life I was at complete peace... a peace I cannot explain in words. My girlfriend stopped by and I told her I did not want her to think I was emotionless and stone-hearted, but I was just sitting in a good place.

The girlfriend took off and I called Mom to see how she was holding up. She said they stabilized Dad and told her to go home to rest, and they would call her if anything happened. She was telling me of a book that she took up and started reading. In the book, the man called the woman, "Fred," just like my dad called my mother.

I told her that was God's way of letting her know she wasn't alone. I told her of the gal I had met, and the wonders of God in this world. She interrupted me to let me go because the hospital was calling. Within seconds of hanging up the phone, I looked up... It felt as if a knife pierced through my heart and tears instantly swelled in my eyes.

Shortly after, I texted and Mom replied back that the news wasn't good, and that God had taken over. Total sympathy to all who receive that info. No matter how tough you think you are, it will stop a grown man in his tracks. I went in and told my son, barely able to utter the words. He came out and gave me a huge hug.

As we came upon the visitation, the family's heart strings were torn, and anger and pain bubbled to the surface. That family meeting that dad was going to call had now become his funeral. Once again, I was getting hit from both sides. In trying to mourn, I was feeling like a ping pong ball. "What do I do, Jeff?" "How do we do this, Jeff?" "What's next, Jeff?"

I asked the church and everyone I knew for prayers, and asked God to use me as a vessel of peace. That in the darkness and the ugliness of seven years of separation, we could all come together to honor our father's life. I felt the anxieties pouring on to me, like a thick oil trying to suffocate me. Each night, I hit my knees and gave the battle to the Lord.

A generational curse staring us directly in the face with unhealed trauma from my mom's days with her father. We were speaking on the phone, and my mom said, "I just wanted my dad to love your dad and I, and to accept our relationship." I said, "Well, how do you think Luke feels? From the get-go, his wife has not felt…."

A loud scream and my mother hung up the phone, furious. At this moment, a hurtful breakthrough happened. I texted her this message:

In the same way you wanted your dad's love and approval of your relationship, your son sits feeling the same way. I am sorry, Mom. I'm not trying to hurt you, but this is the hurt and trauma I speak of. This hurt will be the breakthrough in the healing. It is ugly and dark things that bring hate and resentment to the forefront. You have every right to feel your every emotion. I love you, Luke, Ronda, and especially my father. God does not give us what we can't handle, with Him by our side. We lead to destruction in self-will. I wish there was a quick fix or a snap of the fingers. I faced my demons head on and found a freedom and peace. You never gave up on me and I will not give up on you or my siblings.

After processing some things, my mother ended up texting my brother and his wife. This time, she took fault for herself. I had spoken to her about asking for forgiveness from Christ once, and that in repentance, we ask that God changes us. That we do not keep asking for forgiveness for wrong actions in sin.

We were able to come together and set differences aside to honor our father. I felt God moving. By no means will it be easy, but it is a step in the right direction. My church family surrounded me with love at the visitation. I am grateful for the family I have created within it.

Now… In wrapping this first book up, I end with this… An

old friend reached out to me. We had had a falling out way back, but life had brought us back together. He had battled a rough upbringing and battled addiction. He called me one night and said, "Not sure how to ask this, but you seem to have life together, and got things figured out…" The salt thing…

I answered with this:

For what it is worth, I cannot take much credit for the stability in my life. I surrendered my will to God's, and when I find myself agitated or losing touch, I pray, go to church, hit AA, or call someone. When I start getting a negative mindset, I go over all the blessings in my life to be grateful for.

At the moment, my father is in the ER, my family is still broken where we can't get together, and I barely speak with my daughter. I tend to be looked at as a bank, and that I just need to put my "big boy" pants on, and I am toxic to be around. I'm lucky to see her ten times a year and she only lives twenty minutes away.

After the fall, my body is nothing like what it used to be, and I deal with pain and limited mobility every day. Through it all, it is nothing compared to what Jesus went through in washing us of our sins. I will take physical pain of spiritual brokenness any day of the week.

THE ACTUAL ENDING

Welp... I sit here on 1-20-2024, a year after my father's passing, and still haven't finished this book. I thought that day after the luncheon that I had sat down and finished it, but I came to find out, the story wasn't finished. I mean, what great story of redemption would end with me being in turmoil with my daughter?

Life continued on and the son graduated in May of 2023. I told him I would take him ocean fishing and remained a man of my word. I took him and his buddy down for a two-day guided fishing trip. We had a blast and caught all kinds of fish.

I won't lie. The first day out, the boys were second-guessing life. A storm blew in and we went out farther, thinking we could get out of it. Somehow, the storm shifted direction and seemed to be chasing us. It dropped from 80 degrees and calm water, down to 65 degrees with 6-8ft roller waves and pouring rain. I figured the good Lord wanted to make an adventure out of it. All in all, the weather did its thing and so did we, slaying fish.

One HUGE thing, and one of the coolest things in my life to date, happened in this time. My nonprofit partner that started coming to church started seeing breakthroughs. He went from a completely defeated man, to a man full of smiles who was talking people's ears off. Then one day at church, he ended up getting baptized, and it hit me… How amazing, that through my brokenness, he saw God's light and came to it for himself, to find Jesus Christ.

Fast forward, a bunch of buildings built, a good tan, and Mom's birthday came. We celebrated at her house on the river. My daughter showed up and was civil… until it was time to leave. She took off in her car without saying a word. I sat down in my car, kind of distraught. Next thing you know, she opened up my car door and sat down.

In an attempt to resolve a multitude of issues, things escalated quickly. My daughter was hurt from my past, but also in hell in her current living situation. I tried to offer her the room that my son had at my apartment, but she refused. I asked how I was supposed to help if she rejected my offer.

After a bout of yelling, I lost my cool and yelled at her to get out of my car and stay out of my life. She sped off and I made my way. Instantly, the devil was waiting, lurking in the night. He was on the prowl. Thoughts quickly flooded my head of why I even got sober, and that I should have just stayed in my intoxicated world.

This now grown teenage woman, that used to be Daddy's little princess, was broken, and I didn't know how to fix it. I thought that in getting sober, it would work itself out, but over three years later and here we are, with me yelling in rage for my daughter to stay out of my life. How could that little princess that was once wrapped around my finger hold so much resentment?

I quickly went into prayer and asked the Lord's help. I knew my daughter was hurt and leaning on the world. I knew that I had to stay on the path of righteousness, regardless of how emotionally pinned I felt in that moment. I got home and hit my knees. I gave the battle to the Lord and asked that he keep my daughter safe, but that he reveal to her the truth of her situation.

The following weeks, I dove headfirst into AA meeting and leaning on my church family for prayers. I sat with my pastor and his wife and told my situation to members of jail at my AA talk. That this sobriety thing isn't always sunshine and rainbows. I felt completely defeated. Three years into my sobriety and still no progress with my daughter.

What I didn't know about was the break right before the breakthrough. I apologized to my daughter the next day in a text. I let her know that things didn't go as I would have liked, but that I was putting the ball in her court, and that if she chose that living situation, to live in its truths. I told her I loved her, but wouldn't be taking any part in her living in that situation.

Fast forward about a month… I'm at work and everything was going wrong that day. The steel on a building was ordered wrong, my son and his friend were completely going against my instruction, and then my other worker topped it off by punching the wrong stack of steel, costing about $1,600.00 in material.

I went to grab my phone to get that material shipping with the other steel that we needed. It was then that I saw a text from my daughter…

"I can't explain everything right now, but, Dad, I'm moving in with you"

I about s**t my pants and my heart may have skipped a beat. I slowly returned to the crew, with a huge smile on my face. I looked at my son and said, "Mattie's moving in with me!"

I came to find out that her mom's boyfriend had gotten into a physical altercation with her and she had all she could take. She decided to rekindle our relationship than to live another day in that house with him. I end up rearranging the apartment to accommodate her. I gave her my room and got a bedroom set to fit most of her clothes.

My daughter's fear was that I would constantly bad-talk her mom, and put her in the middle of conversations she didn't want to be part of. I had tried to tell her I was changed, but since she stayed gone, she hadn't seen the man I had become in sobriety.

To say the least, she has made herself a comfy little living quarters, de-stressing from the chaotic living atmosphere she was in. She also took the mic at church and shared her testimony of the hell that her mom's boyfriend had put her through over the years. She had the whole room in tears, and I couldn't have been any prouder of her for taking on the darkness.

To this day, I still share this story at the jail during AA talks. One thinks in getting sober and feeling better that life just instantly gets better. All I can say is that I had three and a half years of time to throw it all away because circumstances weren't what I wanted, but in long-suffering and turning the battle over to the Lord, the missing piece of the puzzle was put in place.

In giving my life to Christ and getting sober, everything I had lost in my life was restored and renewed for the better. I had once told my kids' mother that I would never fight her or try to take these kids from her again, but that her actions would give them back to me. She chose a broken man with money over her kids' best interest, and they came back to me.

THANK YOU, LORD, for my redemption story. For breathing life back into these dry bones. From the pits of hell to my family, finances, health, and whatever else being restored. God is too good not to believe, and this is his work through me.

I have received an anointing over my life to bring hope to others with my story. So, in writing these last words, I reflect on a whirlwind of emotions. I sit at my kitchen, typing on my laptop, just hours after seeing and touching my father for the last time. Some big shoes to fill and a mom that will need my support in moving forward.

Well, that was from the original ending, but... here I still sit, chatting with my mom, as I finish this book on my laptop. I'm overlooking the frozen Cedar River on the one-year anniversary of my father's passing. We are getting together for supper tonight as a reunited family... minus one.

I realize all I can do is operate in God's will for my life, and chase my sobriety with everything I have. Without my sobriety, and God in my life, I am a dead man walking and have nothing. Chasing things of this Earth has not and will not bring purpose to my life. People see my life as being all together, but it is falling into place more because of doing the next right thing. By no means am I perfect, and I still battle with a sinful nature, but I strive to be better each day.

Like they say in AA… **"It's spiritual progress over spiritual perfection."**

There is only one who is perfect, and who saves, heals, restores, renews, and redeems. His name is Jesus Christ, and through him we receive the Father. Like my good friend, Chuck, says, "I'm going to keep showing up and see what happens next!"

I hope you have enjoyed reading my story, and that it has brought hope or inspired you in some way to pick up your own cross and walk with Jesus. We are entering troubled times and there is freedom in his name. May God be with you and be your peace. He has stuck by me through all these trials. There was another in the fire, and the same way that he was awaiting my return, he awaits all of you.

I was shattered, torn, defeated, tired, betrayed, hated, and felt I was BEYOND BROKEN…

Who would want or love this monstrosity? I lifted my hands to the Lord, picked up my cross, and surrendered my life…
I was redeemed, I was restored, and I was renewed…

*I am **BEYOND BROKEN!!!***
*and there is **NO TURNING BACK!!!***

A PAGE OF THANKS

I would like to extend a sincere thank you to all those involved in my redemption and healing journey. First and foremost, my Lord and Savior, Jesus Christ. Through him all things are possible. That when I was at the end of myself, his loving hand was outreached and brought this prodigal son in.

Next, I would like to extend a thank you to my AA and church community. A few personal to Pastor Nate and his father, Scott; my sponsor Don; Carly; LuAnn and Roger; Dave, my business partner and also fellow sober friend; Mr. Baker; and anyone one else who played a supportive role in my recovery journey.

A heartfelt thank you goes out to all the people I met in this book and the staff on board that took care of me when I was in California. Some days I pinch myself wondering if it was all a dream. In a leap of faith, I could sense God all over my time in California.

Lastly, a huge thank you goes out to my family and kids for praying and believing in me through this healing journey. From my sister cleaning my house and making it more a home for my return, to my parents' prayers and financially keeping me afloat, and my brother and his wife taking care of me while in the nursing home after Fall. Not quite the best way to get reunited with family, but it's part of the story. THANK YOU! THANK YOU! THANK YOU!

ABOUT THE AUTHOR

Hello, there! My name is Jeff... (LOL) Just your everyday sinner that was brought back to life from the depths of addiction by the one and only Jesus Christ. Some have given me a super-human complex (might be the fake hip), but in staying humble I'm just a hard-working, small-town guy with a big heart.

I went from a life of living all my time wasted to barely wasting anytime. In being so close to not wanting to live another day that light bulb turned on, to that there is a lot of living I have left to do. Guess they say life is all about perspective.

Anywho... I run a post frame construction company, and I have a nonprofit that runs more like a hobby. It's a small ministry to bring hope to people undergoing unexpected hardship. If I'm not at work I'm typically working on a side project for someone at the church... or taking naps... I love naps.

I currently play acoustic guitar in my praise band at church. I'm active in church life groups and doing AA meetings at the local county jail. I love to cook and when I get the chance, writing music and dabbling in art.

One thing that I never knew about me was that I would be an author one day, sharing my testimony and redemption story with the world, but God had some different plans and now look at me go. I hope my story touches your life and that maybe one day I will see you at a speaking engagement. God bless and thanks for reading!

www.ingramcontent.com/pod-product-compliance
Lightning Source LLC
Chambersburg PA
CBHW021233130626
46554CB00004B/1467